Art of Nature

Three Centuries of Natural History Art
from Around the World

JUDITH MAGEE

Art of Nature

Three Centuries of Natural History Art
from Around the World

Published by the
Natural History Museum, London

First published by the Natural History Museum,
Cromwell Road, London SW7 5BD

© Natural History Museum, 2009

ISBN 978 0 565 09244 3

A catalogue record for this book is
available from the British Library.

Designed by David Mackintosh
Reproduction by Saxon Digital Services
Printing by C & C Offset

PAGE 1 KONRAD GESNER
Historiae Animalium, 1551
Engraving
380 x 240 mm

PAGES 2&3 ROBERT HOOKE
Micrographia, 1665
Engraving
300 x 194 mm

RIGHT ULISSE ALDROVANDI
Roe deer
Capreolus capredus
Engraving, 1642
340 x 235 mm

CONTENTS

INTRODUCTION:
Visions of the Natural World

O F ALL THE SCIENCES natural history lends itself best to being represented through visual media. Whereas words can be abstract, ambiguous, misunderstood or mistranslated, a picture drawn with skill and accuracy portrays a reality everyone can relate to. Drawings, it can be argued, give the visible facts so that words become subordinate to the image. 'Where accurate figures are given,' stated British naturalist George Edwards in 1758, 'much pains may be spared in verbal descriptions'.[1] Yet although natural history illustrators strive to draw specimens as true to life as possible, what they depict is always selective. Variations in scale, manipulation of the subject to conform to design, the placing of the subject with other animals and plants that have no natural connection, and the projection of the artist's own preconceptions about the flora, fauna, landscape and people of other lands inevitably influence natural history art.

From the earliest civilisations plants and animals have been portrayed as a means of understanding and recording their potential uses, such as their economic and healing properties. From the first illustrated catalogue of medicinal plants, *De Materia Medica* by Dioscorides, in the first century, through to the late fourteenth century, the illustration of plants and animals changed very little. Indeed woodcuts in instructional manuals and herbals were often repeatedly copied over the centuries, resulting in a loss of definition and accuracy so that they became little more than stylized decoration. With the growing popularity of copperplate engravings, the traditional use of woodcuts declined and the representation of plants and animals became more accurate. Then, with the emergence of artists such as Albrecht Dürer and Leonardo Da Vinci, naturalists such as Otto Brunfels, Leonhard Fuchs in botany and Konrad Gesner and Ulisse Aldrovandi in zoology, nature began to be depicted in a more realistic style. Individual living plants or animals were observed directly and their likeness rendered onto paper or vellum.

The scientific revolution in seventeenth-century Europe paved the way for voyages of discovery and exploration of the world on a scale never seen before. Men and women took up the challenge of venturing to new and distant lands to discover and bring home bizarre and wonderful plants and animals. The artwork produced by these explorers provides us with a record of how Europeans attempted to make sense of what they were encountering for the first time in these far off lands. Through their artwork they were endeavouring to make known the unusual and the exotic, the rare and the dramatic, to a broader audience that extended beyond the traditional circle of philosophers, physicians and herbalists. For the first time there were artists who dedicated their lives to depicting nature.

As nautical exploration opened up new parts of the world to Europe, the Dutch, British and Spanish soon established a worldwide trading mechanism. Traditional land routes were replaced by transoceanic trade routes and vessels that transported greater quantities of cargo in much less time. With this came an expansion of commerce, the beginnings of industrialization and modern empire building. And so dawned a time of major change in European politics, culture, science and technology, during which rationalism replaced superstition and revelation. European expansion into areas across the globe encouraged and stimulated curiosity about the natural products of these previously unexplored countries and scientific exploration became an important part of this expansion. The interests of commercial companies and governments often coincided with those of scientists and naturalists. The great European powers were maritime nations and they relied on supplies of wood for shipbuilding, plants with medicinal properties and crops that potentially could be grown outside of their native land. A specimen or a drawing was often the key to identification of these plants and so natural history art served not only a taxonomic function for the scientist but also provided information for the decision and policy makers of commerce and government. The first major expeditions to discover the exotic plants of the Americas, India and Africa were undertaken by those in the service of the Spanish and Portuguese empires. Their purpose was to find plants that were considered useful in medicine and to record their location and glean as much information as possible on their supposed virtues from the local inhabitants. Men such as Garcia de Orta in India and Francisco Hernandez in Mexico were amongst the first Europeans to describe accurately the flora and fauna of these parts of the world. And accompanying these men of science were artists instructed to draw the plants and animals of interest.

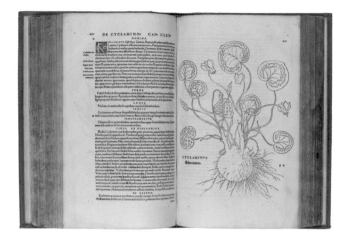

ABOVE Fuchs' *De Historia Stirpium Commentarii Insignes* was one of the first books to include illustrations produced from direct observations of living plants. The drawings set a new standard for illustrating herbals, and natural history books and other artists copied many of the drawings for years afterwards. The original drawings were made by the artist Albrecht Meyer.

LEONHARD FUCHS
De Historia Stirpium Commentarii insignes, 1542
Engraving,
370 x 233 mm

The great surge in natural history illustration, however, began in the late seventeenth century with artists such as Maria Sibylla Merian, and flourished again in the eighteenth century with the celebrated botanical artists such as Georg Ehret and Franz and Ferdinand Bauer and the intrepid traveller artists of the voyages and expeditions of discovery. It continued through to the mid-nineteenth century where it is represented by artists such as John James Audubon, Walter Hood Fitch and John Gould, masters in technique and finish. As natural history art took on a growing significance for science, the importance of detail and accuracy became ever greater. Helpful guides began to appear that gave instruction in drawing and the first colour nomenclature handbooks were published.

For many who chose to travel, their experiences were the realization of their dreams, and the stories of their travels are 'such stuff that dreams are made on' (William Shakespeare *The Tempest*). They contain all the ingredients for fascinating tales: adventure, intrigue, obsession, passion, danger, tragedy, excitement, joy and disappointment. These field naturalists were excellent observers and often very good artists. Some scorned those academics marooned in their studies painstakingly working through the systematics of the specimen. The American ornithologist Alexander Wilson certainly had no time for the closet naturalist and claimed that he had turned a thousand times from 'the barren and musty records' of the systematic writers with a 'delight bordering on adoration, to the magnificent repository of the woods and fields'.[2] It was the traveller naturalists and artists who became heroes in the public eye and to a great extent the public perception of natural science during the eighteenth and nineteenth centuries was defined by travel.

What motivated these artists, collectors and travellers to risk their lives and future livelihood in search of the unknown? Aspirations varied; some sought fame as scientists or artists, some financial

gain or at least the prospect of making a living from what they loved doing. For others it provided the opportunity to present their view of nature to a wider community. The American naturalist William Bartram, who travelled in the southeast of North America, realized not only his own dreams but also those of his father who had for years desired to see the Mississippi River 'the grand Sire of them all'.[3] Whatever the motives, few would have contradicted Alexander Humboldt's comment that he was 'spurred on by an uncertain longing for what is distant and unknown, for whatever excited my fantasy: danger at sea, the desire for adventures, to be transported from a boring daily life to a marvellous world'.[4] Joseph Hooker, who became director of Kew Botanic Gardens, chose to travel to India and the Himalayas because the land was a 'mystery equally attractive to the traveller and the naturalist'.[5] And almost without exception, the scientist, artist, philosopher or dreamer who travelled in the late eighteenth and early nineteenth centuries conducted their work with a view to it being published.

Most of the artists would of course have been unable to travel without some form of financial support, whether an official salary, sponsorship, commissions or even just help with their travelling costs. Support came from an array of individuals, organizations and institutions. Surprisingly few naturalists and even fewer artists were directly funded by the state, although Spanish and French governments were more prepared to put money into exploration than the British. Government-funded artists accompanied Louis de Bougainville's circumnavigation of the globe and Nicolas Baudin's expedition to Australia and also the Spanish expeditions to South America and Mexico. In Britain, government-organized voyages and expeditions were heavily reliant on funding from elsewhere to cover artists' costs. Wealthy patrons and men of influence such as Sir Joseph Banks and institutions such as the Royal Society had, by the end of the eighteenth century, managed to convince British

ABOVE Hans Weiditz produced the woodcuts for Brunfels' botanical works (left). He was one of the first illustrators to draw directly from life. Francisco Hernandez (right) was part of what is considered to be the first scientific expedition to the New World, in 1571, seeking out plants useful to medicine and agriculture.

OTTO BRUNFELS
Cannabis sativa Herbarum Vivae Eiconeb, 1536
Engraving
311 x 190 mm

FRANCISCO HERNANDEZ
Rerum Medicarum Novæ Hispaniæ Thesaurus, 1651
Engraving
330 x 220 mm

RIGHT Franz Bauer produced an enormous body of work during his employment as the first botanical artist at the Royal Botanic Gardens, Kew. One area of illustration that he specialized in was the drawing of plant anatomy from his observations through a microscope. His study of pollen began as early as 1794 and he is considered to be the first artist to accurately draw the germination of pollen cells.

FRANZ BAUER
Pollen grain of Lilium, *Lilium lancifolium*
Watercolour, *c.*1800
240 x 160 mm

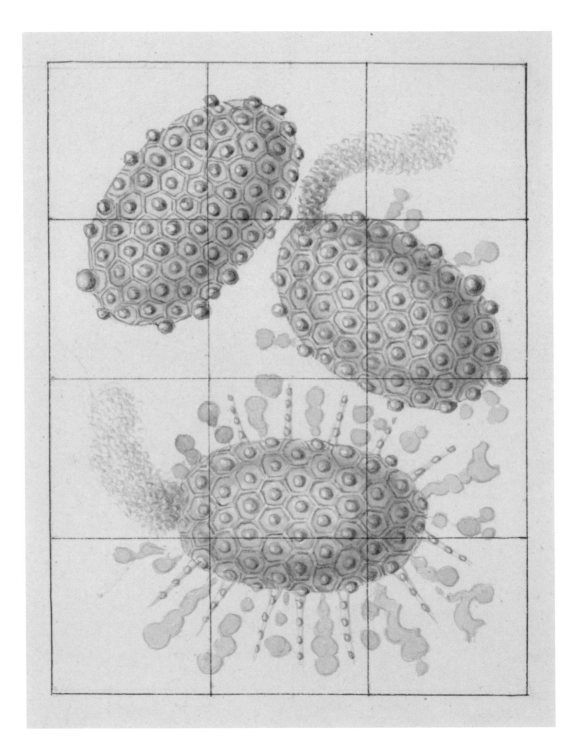

governments of the importance of having a natural history component on expeditions; but more often than not they had to underwrite the costs of this work. For James Cook's second voyage, for example, the Admiralty recognized the advantage of having dedicated artists and naturalists on board. But this view did not always prevail and notable voyages such as that of the First Fleet had no official naturalist or artist on any one of the eleven ships.

There were thus some artists who relied on the state or closely associated institutions such as the Royal Society in Britain or the Académie des Sciences in France to fund their inclusion on an expedition. By the nineteenth century the Royal Geographical Society also funded many artists and naturalists including Robert Schomburgk and Thomas Baines. Others found they could pursue their interest in botany or zoology as paid servants of a commercial institution such as the Dutch or British East India Company or, like William Bartram, rely on the patronage of a wealthy individual. Finally there were those with no external support who either, like Alexander Humboldt, were affluent enough to fund their own adventures or had to support their travels by selling the specimens they collected, as did Alfred Russel Wallace or, like Alexander Wilson, rely on the sale of their published artwork.

For taxonomic purposes natural history art was and remains today an important element in classifying a species. It serves as an aid for the scientists in their work of identification, allowing them to describe, classify and name the thing depicted. Once classified, an illustration can be studied by others, enabling them to know the plant or animal almost at a glance instead of spending hours pouring over written descriptions. This was particularly useful for people in the medical profession, especially when travelling in foreign lands. Recognizing and selecting the correct plant could be the difference between healing or poisoning oneself and others. In botanical illustration the purpose is to show the different stages of development of a plant: in bud, blossom and in fruit. The illustration may also include dissected parts showing the internal structure often drawn at greater magnification. This method of drawing was directly influenced by the work of Carl Linnaeus in the mid-eighteenth century, who stamped his authority on the natural sciences by introducing a classification system based on the sexual characteristics of plants.

Representation of animals can be a more challenging art. For a zoological illustration to be of real service to the scientist it requires realistic morphological appearance together with accurate internal anatomical structures. Artists that remained in Europe often had to rely on their imagination when depicting animals, as the only specimens they had to observe were dead and mangled carcasses. For species that metamorphose through distinct stages, often the whole life-cycle is depicted.

With the development of complex theories about the natural world, the role of natural history art also changed. By the mid-nineteenth century Darwin's and Wallace's theories of natural

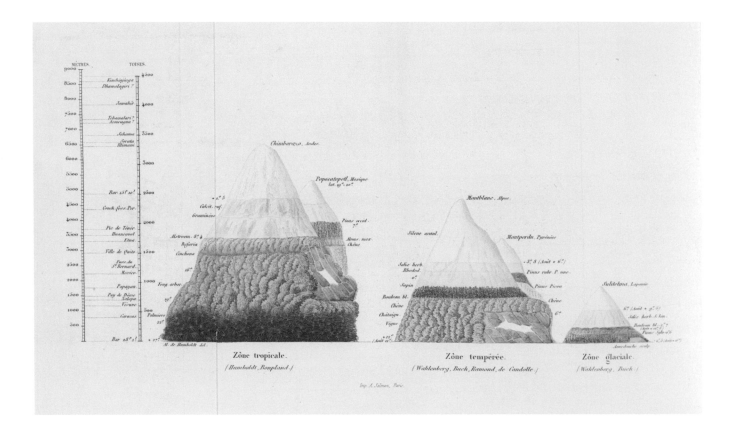

selection were well nigh impossible to illustrate. For other new ideas illustrative diagrams were used. Alexander Humboldt was a master in portraying his system of plant geography through diagrams. Technological progress also led to new ways of looking at things. For centuries instruments have helped capture images not visible to the naked eye and some wonderful examples include Hooke's depiction of the ant and Franz Bauer's drawings of pollen and seed germination, all made with the assistance of a microscope. By the second half of the nineteenth century the microscope enabled artists such as Ernst Haeckel to delineate structures of beautiful marine organisms.

Many of the great collections of natural history art built during the eighteenth and nineteenth centuries are held in eminent institutions of learning and culture throughout Europe. Formed by wealthy individuals, powerful trading companies and various agencies or arms of the state, these collections represent natural history from around the globe. The importance of much of the artwork is enhanced by its association with some of the most significant and momentous events in the history of the natural sciences. These include some of the famous voyages and expeditions of

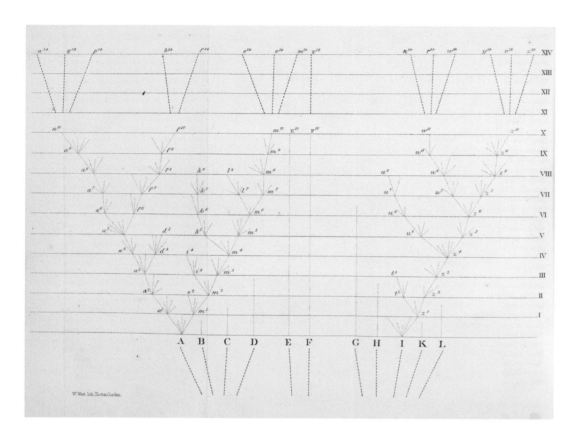

discovery, individual feats of courage and perseverance and the synthesis of ideas into understanding the origins and diversity of all living species.

This book looks at natural history illustration continent by continent. Each has its own special history of collectors and artists that reflects the varying relationships between country and colonizer or visitor. This history is also often symptomatic of the opinions held by Europeans of these unknown and far off lands and their people. The expectations they had for the future of these lands, of how they should be understood and explained, all contributed to the varying impressions and interpretations produced by artists and naturalists of the places they visited. It is for these reasons the art is very much a view of the natural world from a European perspective and can reveal as much about European cultural history as it does of the natural history it depicts.

The Am

HERNANDEZ **WHITE** MERIAN **CATESBY** BARTRAM **YOUNG** ABBOTT **WILSON**

ericas

DUBON **HUMBOLDT** FORSTER **PARKINSON** WALLACE **BATES** SCHOMBURGK

THE AMERICAS:

Discovering and Recording the New World

E UROPEAN PRESENCE IN THE AMERICAS began in the fifteenth century with the emerging Spanish and Portuguese empires. France and England established themselves in areas of North America by the late sixteenth century and, by the early eighteenth century, a further five European countries held territory in the New World. The impact of European colonization of the Americas was immense, changing significantly the landscape, people, flora and fauna of the continents. By the last quarter of the eighteenth century challenge to colonial rule was growing, with the first successful revolution taking place in the British colonies in 1776. The beginning of the nineteenth century witnessed a mounting ferment of nationalism amongst the different regions of the Spanish empire, resulting in the creation of more than a dozen nation states by 1825. The break from European domination had far reaching consequences in the field of natural history. The newly formed Republic of the United States of America sought to establish itself as an independent country in all areas of public life. There were many amongst the scientific community who thought that Americans should no longer rely on Europeans to collect, describe and interpret the natural products of their country. Thomas Jefferson stated that in the field of natural history Americans had 'done too little for [themselves] and depend[ed] too long on the ancient and inaccurate observation of other nations'.[1] The concern was that natural history should be an all American activity that would contribute to the forging of a new nation.

Some of the first natural history illustrations to emerge as a result of European presence in the Americas include drawings prepared by indigenous artists for Francisco Hernández during his seven year expedition to Mexico in 1571; drawings by John White in 1587 from the English settlement at Roanoke Island, and the magnificent depictions of Surinam plants and insects by Maria Sibylla Merian a century later. Merian was one of the first artists to travel and produce watercolours of tropical plants, insects and other animals that were then transferred to engravings for published works. They were published as *Metamorphosis insectorum Surinamensium* in 1705, a work that expressed something quite new in natural history art – her colour plates were the first to show the habitat of the fauna and the inter-relationship between plants and insects.

Merian was an extraordinary woman by any century's standards. In 1699 she sailed to the Dutch colony in Surinam to study and paint the insects that had captured her interest as a young child. She succeeded in publishing scientific works and was a well-respected naturalist amongst the leading European experts of the day. As such, her artwork was sought after by some of the most powerful and wealthiest heads of state. Merian's knowledge of the subjects she painted was outstanding and she developed an in-depth understanding of the complexities of the life-cycle of many insects. She was fascinated by the metamorphosis of moths and butterflies, from egg to caterpillar and from chrysalis to adult. She recorded all these stages in her paintings and included the plants that the insects fed upon. Her scientific study of insects is even more remarkable considering how little was known of the subject in the late seventeenth century. The term entomology was not coined until the mid-eighteenth century and very few texts had been published on the subject by the time Merian crossed the Atlantic.

MARIA SIBYLLA MERIAN
Metamorphosis Insectorum Surinamensium,
1726 edition
Hand-coloured engraving,
525 x 555 mm

Merian financed her journey to Surinam by selling her many paintings and natural history collections and risked her future in order to embark on a wonderful adventure. Merian's works, although published, would have been seen only by the select few who could afford the purchase of such large folio volumes, or who had access to those owned by wealthy friends or scientific institutions such as the Royal Society. Her influence, nevertheless, was significant amongst those interested in natural history and its art.

One man fortunate enough to see a set of her original watercolours, and who was most certainly inspired by them, was Mark Catesby. Like Merian, Catesby was not wealthy and was reliant on others to support his travels, studies and publishing venture. In 1712 he left his home in Suffolk to cross the Atlantic to Williamsburg in Virginia where he spent seven years travelling, drawing and collecting plant specimens. Catesby returned to England in 1719, eager to build on the wealth of knowledge he had acquired about the natural history of the New World . He was introduced to the distinguished botanist William Sherard, who was impressed with Catesby's enthusiasm and drawing ability and was looking for someone to take up an offer by the Governor of South Carolina to draw plants and animals from the region. The offer came with an annual allowance of £20 but further funds were needed to pay Catesby's passage. The post also required the support of the Royal Society. The recommendation was not hard to obtain but the Royal Society was not prepared to offer funding so individual backers had to be found. A syndicate was formed including, amongst others, Sherard and Sir Hans Sloane and, with funding in place, Catesby set sail once again to North America in 1722.

Catesby's second visit lasted four years. He collected specimens, made drawings and sketches of unknown flora and fauna and sent regular boxes of seed and animal specimens to his benefactors. South Carolina was at that time one of the frontier British colonies and his travels were fraught with danger. Not only was he exploring a country that was wild and unknown to Europeans but he also risked attack from unwelcoming Native Americans. Catesby returned to England in 1726 already determined to publish his drawings of living plants and animals that he had observed in the wild. He dedicated the next 17 years to this project, preparing the plates for his magnificent two-volume work *The Natural History of Carolina, Florida and the Bahama Islands*, published between 1731 and 1743. Having taken lessons in engraving he proceeded to make the plates for his work, thereby reducing the almost prohibitive cost of production. As with his travels, Catesby would never have been able to complete this work without the support of patrons. In this case it was Peter Collinson, a Quaker merchant dealing in fabrics and living in London, who provided the funds.

Collinson was passionate about plants and kept his own splendid garden which he stocked with rare and exotic plants from around the world. Catesby's volumes were the first to depict many of these new plants and birds from America and Collinson was eager to have such a work available. He agreed to lend Catesby a fairly large sum of money, free of interest that would enable him to publish his work. Snakes, amphibians, insects, mammals, birds and plants all figure in Catesby's illustrations. The plates are a curious mixture of splendour, humour, attention to detail and inaccuracies. Many of the birds and smaller creatures are life size and are placed in natural settings true to their habitat; whilst for some subjects the scale has been disregarded and the relationship between species and background flora and landscape is a fabrication. The influence of Merian on Catesby's work is clearly visible. Catesby was by no means as skilled an artist as Merian but his work contains a vitality that is just as pleasing.

Catesby's *Natural History of Carolina, Florida and the Bahamas* was a pioneering work and was closely followed by George Edwards' *A Natural History of Uncommon Birds,* a multi-volume work that included birds and other creatures from around the world. The illustrations earned Edwards the Gold Medal of the Royal Society. Edwards had travelled extensively as a young man, drawing and observing nature, but he also relied on specimens and drawings from his wide range of contacts with naturalists, sailors and settlers around the world. One important contributor to Edwards' work was an enthusiastic young American, William Bartram. William was the son of John Bartram, a nurseryman and farmer from Philadelphia, who supplied seed of North American plants to the keen gardeners of Europe and who, in 1765, was appointed the King's Botanist. From the age of 12 William Bartram accompanied his father on many of his plant collecting expeditions. On these excursions the 'little

OPPOSITE John White was recruited as artist for Walter Raleigh's 1585 expedition to the New World. His drawings of the natural history of what is now North Carolina are the earliest surviving European record of the indigenous people and flora and fauna of the New World. The instructions to White are now lost but similar ones for artists at this time include drawing all 'strange birdes beastes fishes plantes hearbes trees and fruites'. Many of the drawings that White prepared were published in 1590 by Theodor de Bry.

JOHN WHITE
Fishing scene
Hand-coloured engraving,
c.1580s
367 x 250 mm

OPPOSITE William Bartram influenced American and European scientists and also inspired many European Romantic poets. Both William Wordsworth and Samuel Taylor Coleridge borrowed heavily from Bartram's writings to describe the landscape, plants and animals for their own poetry. It was Bartram's view of nature, as a living unity of diverse and interdependent life forms, one organic, harmonious whole, which captured the poets' imagination. Much of Bartram's writings and many of his drawings communicate a sense of the sublime of the natural world.

WILLIAM BARTRAM
Green-backed heron,
Butorides striatus
Thalia sp. (plant)
Black ink and watercolour,
[1774]
377 x 245 mm

botanist', as his father called him, learnt about birds, animals, plants, minerals and the structure of the Earth, making accurate drawings of what he observed in nature. Although he never received any formal tuition in drawing he had a perceptive eye and learnt to draw by studying the engraved plates in the books by Catesby and Edwards. This raw gift combined with a love and understanding of nature meant that he soon developed a skilled and artistic hand.

In 1765 John and William Bartram spent ten months exploring the flora and fauna of Georgia and Florida. This first encounter with Florida instilled in William an everlasting love of the 'delightful country, that he often fancied himself transported thither in his dreams by night'.[2] The opportunity to return there came in 1773, after he persuaded the physician John Fothergill of London to become his patron. For almost four years he travelled through the Carolinas, Georgia and Florida and as far as the Mississippi River, collecting plants and seed, drawing and keeping a journal. He travelled with traders and Native Americans, observing their lifestyle, culture and language. Today he is known for his *Travels through North and South Carolina, Georgia and Florida*, published in 1791, which tells of his adventures. Encounters with 'thunderous roaring' alligators and wild bears when camping along the river-banks were dangerous experiences and Bartram had a narrow escape on more than one occasion. During the American Revolution he became no stranger to the disputes between British troops and rebels in Georgia, taking part in at least one skirmish. Revolutionary activity, however, was not something sought by Bartram and, despite being a firm patriot of the new Republic, by the end of 1776 he decided that his plant-collecting days in the region were over and set off on the long journey to his home in Kingsessing, Philadelphia.

William Bartram was content in his contemplation of the natural world. He dedicated his life to this study and his observations of nature led him to discover the often hidden relationships within it. His comprehension of the delicate balance between species that were interdependent upon each other heralded the study of ecology in the mid-nineteenth century. Bartram's time spent observing and living amongst the Native American peoples gave him an understanding of the harmony that exists between all living things, an understanding that he continued to appreciate throughout his life.

Bartram's drawings contrast interestingly with those of his neighbour, William Young, who was three years his junior and of a very different character. Young was a daring, bumptious, over confident and above all ambitious young man determined to make a living equal to that of John Bartram, by collecting and selling plants and seed. By a stroke of audacity and an added helping of luck, Young managed to secure the favour and patronage of the Queen of England, the German-born Charlotte of Strelitz, and wife of George III. William Young was the son of German immigrants and it was these origins that helped win the favour of Queen Charlotte. She brought him to London to be

Fig 1.

2.

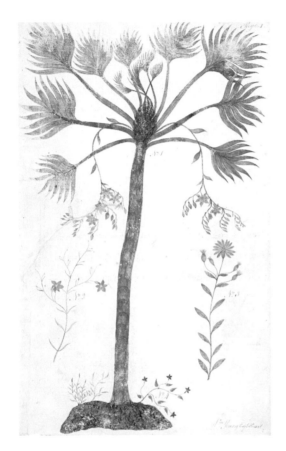

taught botany and bestowed on him the title of Queen's Botanist and a salary of £300 a year. Young's dedication to becoming successful was not mirrored in his application in the study of botany. There were far too many attractions on the fringes of court for him to spend much time looking at dissected plants. Pleasure was expensive and it was not long before Young found himself in debt and in jail. Eventually the Queen arranged for his release, and Young was placed on board a ship bound for his home across the Atlantic and advised by the Queen's agents to remain in America.

On his return to his homeland Young was determined to justify his continued receipt of Crown money. He spent the year of 1767 travelling through North and South Carolina, plant collecting and painting the plants which would be added to the Queen's herbarium. With a flippant disregard for the instructions to remain in America, Young set sail for Britain in 1768 with his specimens, drawings and over 100 living plants. Included in this cargo were several Venus flytraps, which at that stage had not been described or named. For years botanists, gardeners and naturalists had been tantalized by the descriptions of this exciting new plant; it had taken many years to cultivate and it did not travel well. Young was the first to bring the living plant to Europe whilst John Bartram was the first to cultivate the plant in his greenhouse.

William Young established a routine of collecting and dispatching plants to customers and during the American Revolution and War of Independence he moved his business interests to France. In 1785, while out plant collecting at Gunpowder Creek, Maryland, Young tragically fell from a height into the creek below, where he drowned. It was a sad end for one who had brought an element of excitement and daring to the plant-collecting world.

There were several European Naturalists who visited the British Colonies in North America, one of whom was John Abbot. In 1773 at the age of 22 he abandoned his career in law and set sail from Deal in Kent, England for the colony of Virginia. Abbot's aim was to discover new and interesting insects, a subject that had fascinated him from childhood, which he could sell on the European market. As a young boy he demonstrated a talent for drawing and had received art lessons from the engraver Jacob Bonneau. His learning was put to good use as an adult and his paintings became sought after by connoisseurs of natural history art. When he left the shores of Britain for America, Abbott had every intention of returning to his homeland and family. But like many travellers he never left his adopted country and eventually settled in Georgia until his death, aged 89. Abbot was one whose livelihood was made by collecting and painting, but even he, once married and with a child, had to supplement his income by teaching.

Abbot never met with William Bartram although they were both in Georgia in 1776 and their paths may have crossed at some point. It was a time of turmoil, 'times that try men's souls' as Thomas Paine wrote, and both Bartram and Abbot were seeking shelter from the violence. Abbot settled in Burke County, northwest of Savannah and Bartram spent the summer in Darien gathering seed from plants such as *Franklinia* before leaving Georgia altogether later in the year. The two collectors did have contact in later years through a mutual friend and fellow naturalist, Alexander Wilson, the Scottish born author of *American Ornithology*, the first work to describe and depict the birds of America. Alexander Wilson had come under the wing of William Bartram in the early 1800s. It was Bartram who taught Wilson about birds and gave him lessons in how to draw his 'little feathered friends'. Like Bartram, Wilson was a committed supporter of the new Republic and in 1804 petitioned the government to become a citizen. He argued strongly for American scientists to sever their dependence on European naturalists declaring that 'It remains now with Americans themselves to decide, whether they will still send across the Atlantic for an account of the productions of their own country, or become, like every other enlightened people, the proper historians of their own territories'.[3]

Wilson had arrived in America in 1794 having fled poverty and the threat of incarceration in Paisley, Scotland. There he had eked out a poor living as a weaver and itinerant salesman and while travelling through the countryside wrote poetry, studied nature and played his violin or flute. Wilson was an admirer of Thomas Paine, author of *The Rights of Man*, and was a passionate defender of the exploited and downtrodden weavers. It was this fervour that landed him in trouble with the authorities on several occasions. He expressed his radical politics in the form of poetry that he had printed and distributed. After a short stay in prison and the threat of possible transportation, Wilson decided to leave his native land for the freedom of the New World.

Life in his newly adopted country was certainly no bed of roses for Wilson, but he did eventually find work teaching in a school a few miles from Kingsessing. In 1804 he made the momentous decision to abandon the security of paid employment and embark on what became his life's work of recording the birds of America. He spent the last nine years of his life on expeditions through the states of America, walking much of the way, collecting and observing birds, many unknown to science at the time, whilst also trying to raise subscriptions for his books. He would return to Kingsessing for summer periods where he would reside at the Bartram house, recoup his energies, be entertained with conversations of travels and receive drawing instructions from his much loved

OPPOSITE Young's drawings show little artistic training, and are unsophisticated and naïve in style, similar to early herbals. Young made no attempt to draw the different parts of the plant or the transverse sections that would assist in identification. This palm is a native of the southernmost region of North Carolina and is depicted here with several epiphytes.

WILLIAM YOUNG
Cabbage palmetto,
Sabal palmetto
Watercolour, 1768
378 x 234 mm

mentor. Many years of endless toil, poverty and poor diet, however, took its toll and in 1813 Wilson succumbed to a bout of dysentery that claimed his life. Aged 47, he had struggled most of his life against many odds but had in those last nine years at least found some contentment in his study of birds and his friendship with William Bartram.

Wilson's *American Ornithology* was the first of its kind but was overshadowed by a magnificent work published some 20 years later. This was *Birds of America* by John James Audubon, admired then, as it is today, for the life-size portraits of birds that animate its pages. Wilson and Audubon met just the once in Louisville, Kentucky, where Audubon was living at the time. Wilson was on one of his longer expeditions and arrived in Louisville seeking subscribers for his book. Audubon showed him some of his paintings and Wilson wrote that he thought these crayon drawings very good, but he failed to receive support from Audubon for his own work.

Audubon decided not to subscribe to Wilson's work, considering his own artistry far superior to that of Wilson's. Wilson left Audubon a disappointed man and bidding adieu to Louisville he entered in his diary that 'Science and literature has not one friend in this place'. He continued his opinion of the town in a letter to his engraver, Alexander Lawson, writing 'Everyman here is so intent on making of money, that they have neither time nor disposition for improvements'.[4]

Audubon is considered one of the greatest bird artists, famous for his double elephant-folio size volumes published between 1827 and 1838. His plates broke new ground in abandoning the traditional 'magpie and stump' manner of portraying birds. He set his birds in a background of their own habitat and visually described the dynamics of their everyday struggle for survival, depicting them in motion, often in flight or in pursuit of prey. These plates were not meant for scientists working to describe and identify species. They were intended to create an impact on the viewer and provide him or her with an awe-inspiring sense of American wildlife, and they did exactly that.

Audubon spent many months each year travelling through the North American countryside observing, shooting and painting birds. He struggled for most of his life to make a successful business of one kind or another and it was only when the publication of *Birds of America* was completed that he at last had an income to support his family. By this time he was 53 years of age and the best part of his life had passed. In 1843 he embarked on his last project, a three-volume work with colour plates of the mammals of America, *Viviparous Quadrupeds of North America*. This took him travelling once again out west but he soon began to show signs of failing health. By 1848 this had declined to the point were he could no longer paint and his mind was 'all in ruins'. Audubon remained with his family in New York and it was here that he died in 1851. His son, John, executed many of the plates for the volumes and the Reverend John Backman wrote the text. John Backman was an American naturalist who corresponded with most of those active in science in the early nineteenth century. In 1804 he participated in one of the highlights of the year in Philadelphia by attending a dinner organized by the leading scientists in the city, and held at the Peale Museum of Natural History. The dinner was in honour of the German naturalist Alexander Humboldt who was visiting Philadelphia on his return journey from South America to Paris. Humboldt had spent five years travelling through South America, Mexico and the Caribbean. Amongst the naturalists attending the dinner were William Bartram and Alexander Wilson. No record exists as to the conversation between Humboldt and Bartram, so we can only speculate that there must have been a great respect and rapport between them, as their view of nature in which everything is connected and the world seen as an organic whole, was very similar.

Humboldt was born in Berlin in 1769 into a minor aristocratic family, and from his childhood he dreamed of travelling the globe in the footsteps of his heroes Louis de Bougainville and James Cook, who had spent time in the New World on each of his three voyages. Humboldt studied under some of the leading intellectuals of Europe at the universities of Frankfurt an der Oder and Göttingen. It was there that he met with Georg Forster, the artist and assistant naturalist from Captain Cook's second voyage. Forster proved to be a significant influence on Humboldt, who described him as his 'guiding star'. It was with Forster that he had his first taste of scientific exploration when he accompanied him on his travels along the Rhine through France and to England in 1790. After university Humboldt spent five years as an inspector for the Prussian Department of Mines, building on his knowledge of geology and mineralogy. In his spare time he pursued the study of botany and zoology and conducted experiments in animal electricity.

Humboldt embarked upon his five-year expedition to South and Central America in 1799 with the French botanist Aimé Bonpland. He financed his expedition through the inheritance received after the death of his mother. By then he had become a brilliant linguist, possessed an extensive knowledge of all areas of natural history and was also an extremely healthy and fit man. His capacity to climb higher, go further and persist longer at a task than most men was extraordinary. He took with him the most technically up-to-date scientific instruments that enabled him to make astronomic observations and take measurements of gases, liquids and solids, sea temperatures at different depths variations in the Earth's magnetism and the electricity in the atmosphere. Humboldt and Bonpland spent five years penetrating rainforests and crossing the plains and mountains of Venezuela, Colombia, Peru, Ecuador, Mexico and the island of Cuba. They mapped the land and charted the course of the Orinoco and Negro rivers. They climbed mountains and explored the Amazon basin, discovering,

OPPOSITE The plates of Audubon's *Birds of America* were published in sets of five. In most of these sets at least two of the plates encompassed the whole page with dramatic scenes from nature. The remaining three plates depicted the smaller birds such as this hooded warbler.

JOHN JAMES AUDUBON
Hooded warbler,
Wilsonia citrina
Birds of America, 1827–38
Hand-coloured engraving
985 x 650 mm

RIGHT Humboldt and Bonpland travelled for many days on a raft of this type, transporting all their scientific equipment and the large collection of live animals Humboldt accumulated during the course of his travels. Humboldt described the design of the raft as one that Peruvians had 'used since earliest time, for fishing and the transport of goods'. The fruit depicted on the raft provides the viewer with examples of produce from the Equinoxial, or tropical, region.

ALEXANDER HUMBOLDT
Radeau de la Riviere de Guayaquil
Vues des Cordillères, 1810
Hand-coloured engraving
400 x 570 mm

collecting and describing plants and animals new to science. Today Humboldt is recognized as the father of several branches of science including ecology and plant geography.

In July 1801 Humboldt arrived in Bogotá where he met and stayed with Spain's greatest botanist, Jose Celestino Mutis. Mutis arrived in South America from Spain in 1761 as the private physician to the Viceroy of New Granada (northern South America). In 1783 he led the Royal Botanical Expedition, one of the first explorations of the flora and fauna of the region. The expedition was funded over a 25-year period and was assisted by a successive series of artists who depicted the newly discovered plants in over 5,000 drawings. During his stay in Bogotá, Humboldt made a map of the Rio Grande de la Magdalena and presented a copy of it to Mutis before he left. Humboldt was an accomplished artist himself and made drawings of the specimens and provided detailed sketches for other artists to draw and engrave the plates, which accompanied his many volumes of text, for his *Vues des Cordillères*. Some of these plates are wonderful romantic topographical images showing splendid geological formations and the beauty of the settings. A striking feature of these plates is that Humboldt always placed himself and Bonpland somewhere within the scene, linking the observer to what is recorded and observed and confirming that, because Humboldt was there, what the viewer sees is accurate.

Humboldt's reputation preceded him; the newspapers in Europe reported on his adventures long before his return so that when he finally arrived in Paris in August 1804 he was already famous and had secured a scientific reputation of international status. He was now as famous as one of his heroes, Captain James Cook. After he returned to Paris Humboldt wrote over 30 volumes about his travels, one of which is *Personal Narrative*, considered one of the greatest travel books of this period of natural science. The book sold in its thousands and influenced a whole generation of would-be adventurers.

Amongst those who found inspiration in Humboldt's work were two future scientists, Charles Darwin and Alfred Russel Wallace. Charles Darwin sailed as gentleman companion to Captain Robert FitzRoy on the survey ship HMS *Beagle* and, similarly to Joseph Banks on the *Endeavour*, had to pay his passage and living expenses for the privilege. The voyage lasted five years, the main purpose of which was to survey the coast of South America. Alfred Russel Wallace, 14 years Darwin's junior, also travelled to South America, inspired by reading Humboldt's work. In contrast to Darwin, Wallace came from a struggling middle class family. His early working life found him travelling around England wherever the work would take him as an apprentice surveyor to his older brother. Wallace's thirst for knowledge led him to the public libraries and working men's Mechanics' Institutes where he educated himself and later others by giving science lectures.

In his mid-twenties Wallace had become so enraptured with natural history he decided to make it his career. On 26 April 1848, with his friend Walter Henry Bates, he left Liverpool for South America and then spent four years travelling along the Amazon and Negro rivers, collecting birds, insects and plants and recording his findings, writing journals and drawing what he saw. The funding for his travels came from collecting natural history specimens to sell through his agent, Samuel Stephens, in London. Wallace was now 25 years of age and his understanding of the natural sciences had led him to contemplate the more complex issues of biological diversity and the mechanism for evolution. He hoped to find some of the answers during his travels. Wallace collected many specimens and sent regular packages to Stephens, but the bulk of his personal collection, duplicates of those he sold, plus his journals, drawings and live animals travelled with him. On the 12th July 1852 Wallace

OPPOSITE Margaret Mee took a great interest in the conservation of Brazil's rainforests and was active in raising awareness about the biodiversity of the Amazonian region. This was helped by her magnificent watercolour drawings of the plants of the region, such as the bromeliad depicted here. Bromelias are native to the tropical areas of America.

MARGARET MEE
Calaguata, *Bromelia anticantha*
Watercolour and bodycolour, 1958
663 x 481 mm

set sail for Britain from Para in Brazil on the brig *Helen*. After 28 days at sea, Wallace was alerted to a fire on board the ship. He managed to salvage a few items, some coins, shirts and four volumes of drawings of fish from the Rio Negro. Everything else he owned went up in smoke. Wallace and the crew spent ten days in an open boat before being rescued by the *Jordeson*, in which he eventually reached England.

Another to follow in Humboldt's footsteps was Robert Hermann Schomburgk who was born in Freiburg in Saxony in 1804. He travelled through the interior from Essequibo to Esmeralda on the Orinoco in South America some 30 years later. He was yet another traveller dedicated to the study of nature who at first had to finance his own travels to discover new and rare products of nature. In 1831 he conducted a survey of the shoreline of Anegada in the Virgin Islands and published his report in the *Journal of the Royal Geographical Society of London*. This brought him recognition so that in 1835 he was able to secure the support of the Royal Geographical Society for an expedition to South America. Schomburgk stated that it was 'science alone' that led him to British Guiana, present day Guyana, and it was here that he spent four years exploring the region and the borderlines of its neighbouring countries, Venezuela and Brazil.

Upon his return to Europe Schomburgk submitted a report to the British Government on the geographical description of British Guiana, which was later published. He returned to British Guiana, but this time under the authority of the Colonial Office for which he conducted surveys and determined the boundary line of the country. In 1840 Schomburgk's brother, Richard, joined him as the botanist to the expedition and together they explored the natural history of the country. Robert had already made a name for himself as a plant hunter with the discovery of a magnificent giant water lily, *Victoria amazonica* that he sent to Britain in 1837. Although he was German born, Robert Schomburgk continued to serve the British Government until 1864 as British Consul, first in the Dominican Republic and later in Bangkok. In 1844 he received a knighthood from Queen Victoria and he also had conferred on him a Gold Medal from the Royal Geographical Society. He had gone from financing his own travels, to being sponsored by the Royal Geographical Society, to directly serving as a high-ranking agent for the British Government.

Exploration of the Amazon rainforests in the twentieth century continued to attract many natural history artists, one of whom was the intrepid Margaret Mee. Her discoveries of previously unidentified plants and her beautiful watercolour depictions of them have been a major contribution to science. Her work was significant in that it alerted the scientific community to the rapid deforestation that she witnessed during her 32-year residence in Brazil.

Margaret Mee

Bromelia anticantha
Bertol. "Caraguatá"
Represa Billings, S. Paulo
flowered November 1958

By 1685 Maria Merian had joined the Labadist Church, which had a community in La Providence in Surinam. It was there that Merian stayed during her travels in Surinam in 1699. Field trips into the forests for collecting, observing and painting were strewn with difficulties, in particular passing through the dense vegetation. On her return to Amsterdam Merian embarked on producing a folio-sized book with engraved plates based on her watercolours of the insects and associated plants of Surinam. It was to be published 'for the pleasure of scholars and amateurs' and provide them with a wondrous impression of the tropics of the New World.

MARIA SIBYLLA MERIAN
Mucuna (opposite)
Papaya, *Carica papaya* (left)
Metamorphosis insectorum Surinamensium,
1726 edition
Hand-coloured engravings
525 x 555 mm

LEFT The head of this heron is placed with several beetles, a cockroach, a flea and a salamander. Catesby's work was of major importance in the development of scientific art. He was the first to depict birds in association with the plants or animals upon which they fed. In the caption to this drawing Catesby wrote that this bird ate fish, frogs and lizards. The two volumes that make up the *Natural History of Carolina* served as a visual reference and source of the natural history of the southeast region of North America, for Europeans throughout the eighteenth century.

MARK CATESBY
Species uncertain but has been identified as great blue heron, *Ardea herodias*
The Natural History of Carolina, Florida and the Bahama Islands, 1731–1743
Hand-coloured engraving
531 x 360 mm

OPPOSITE AND RIGHT

A small number of Catesby's
plates were copies of
paintings made by John
White in the 1580s when
he visited Roanoke Island.
The botanical artist Georg
Ehret produced two other
plates, depicting plants.
Otherwise the remainder of
the 220 colour plates were
made by Catesby based on
his original field drawings
and observations of live
or preserved specimens in
England. Catesby depicted
a total of one hundred and
nine species of birds, which
figured more than any other
subject from the animal
kingdom. 'I believe very
few Birds have escaped my
knowledge' he wrote in the
preface to his work.

MARK CATESBY
Little blue heron (right),
Egretta caerulea
Greater flamingo (opposite),
Phoenicopterus ruber
*The Natural History of
Carolina, Florida and the
Bahama Islands*, 1731–1743
Hand-coloured engraving
531 x 360 mm

Phænicopterus.

Keratophiton &c.

Turdus Rhomboidelis

Turdus &c

MARK CATESBY
Tang fish, *Acanthurus
coeruleus*
Yellow fish, *Paranthias
furcifer* (left)
Ivory-billed woodpecker,
Campephilus principalis
(right)
*The Natural History of
Carolina, Florida and the
Bahama Islands*, 1731–1743
Hand-coloured engraving
531 x 360 mm

LEFT AND ABOVE Catesby was an early champion of the idea that a good representation of a plant or animal was more able to convey knowledge about the species than text alone. In the preface to his work he stated that, 'The Illuminating Natural History is so particularly essential to the perfect understanding of it, that I may aver a clearer Idea may be conceived from the Figures of Animals and Plants in their proper colours, than from the most exact Description without them.'

38

Franklinia alatamaha.   *A beautiful flowering tree.*

discovered growing near the banks of the R. Alatamaha in Georgia.

Gordonia pubescens   *Received from Will.ᵐ Bartram. Delin.*
1780.

OPPOSITE This drawing of Franklinia meets all the requirements of a botanical illustration. It is a style of drawing often referred to as the Linnaean method, or convention for illustration in which, as Joseph Banks stated, 'each figure is intended to answer itself every question a botanist can wish to ask, respecting the structure of the plant it represents'. Franklinia is today extinct in the wild and it is due to Bartram that it has survived in cultivation.

WILLIAM BARTRAM
Franklinia, *Franklinia alatamaha*
Watercolour, 1788
478 x 354 mm

ABOVE Bartram drew this plant after receiving a branch of a cultivated species from Mr Alexander, who was one of the first American-born professional gardeners, working for the then Proprietor of Pennsylvania, Thomas Penn. In the text accompanying the drawing Bartram described the tubercles of this bitter melon as 'disclosing a scene of still greater beauty and wonder'.

WILLIAM BARTRAM
Balsam pear, *Momordica charanita*
Watercolour, [1769]
295 x 398 mm

RIGHT In his book about his travels in Florida where Bartram first observed this fish, he described it as 'a most beautiful creature… a warrior in a gilded coat of mail'. The legend beneath this drawing states, 'Great Yellow Bream call'd Old Wife of St Johns E Florida'. Bartram was the first to publish a description of the Warmouth in 1791 and the drawing serves as the type specimen, predating by decades any preserved specimen.

WILLIAM BARTRAM
Warmouth, *Lepomis gulosus*
Watercolour and black ink, 1774
198 x 294 mm

Summer Duck.

Passenger Pigeon.

OPPOSITE AND LEFT

John Abbot was very much aware of the changes taking place in nature during his lifetime. He expressed concern over the declining population of birds and insects as a result of agricultural practices and an increasing human population. Many species of insects and birds painted by Abbot are today extinct or endangered, such as the passenger pigeon depicted here.

JOHN ABBOT
Wood duck, *Aix sponsa*
Watercolour, 1827
305 x 190 mm

JOHN ABBOT
Passenger pigeon,
Ectopistes migratorius
Watercolour, 1827
305 x 190 mm

RIGHT Once the production of *American Ornithology* was set in motion, Alexander Wilson spent months each year travelling through the states of America in search of new birds to describe and paint, and to raise subscriptions for his work. His travels brought him into contact with other keen ornithologists who would supply him with specimens and drawings of their own, one of whom was John Abbot. Wilson managed to have a small army of suppliers of bird specimens and information so that he was able to write to a friend that, 'scarcely a wren or tit shall be able to pass along, from New York to Canada, but I shall get intelligence of it'.

ALEXANDER WILSON
Little blue heron, *Egretta caerulea*
Snowy egret, *Egretta thula*
Virginia rail, *Rallus limicola*
Clapper rail, *Rallus longirostris*
American Ornithology, 1824
Hand-coloured engraving
346 x 267 mm

OPPOSITE Wilson's time spent tramping through the country was gruelling and he endured many hardships in unpleasant conditions. At times he was laid low by finding no subscribers to his work despite letters of introduction to a host of potential buyers. After his five days at Louisville, where he met with Audubon but failed to get his support, he travelled on to Lexington, where his spirits were lifted after he managed to raise 15 subscribers. He then journeyed on to Nashville and to the Mississippi region where he visited the site of the death, in 1809, of Meriwether Lewis, of the Lewis and Clark Expedition. Another uplifting incident was the warm welcome he received from Thomas Jefferson at the President's House in Washington. Jefferson had been one of the first to subscribe to Wilson's work in 1807 writing to him that he 'salutes Mr. Wilson with great respect'.

ALEXANDER WILSON
Roseate spoonbill, *Ajaia ajaja*
American avocet, *Recurvirostra americana*,
Sanderling, *Calidris alba*
Semi-palmated sandpiper, *Calidris pusilla*
American Ornithology, 1824
Hand-coloured engraving
346 x 267 mm

ALEXANDER WILSON
Common nighthawk, *Chordeiles minor*
American Ornithology, 1811
Hand-coloured engraving
346 x 267 mm

RIGHT Unable to find a suitable engraver and publisher in America, Audubon travelled to Britain in 1826 with more than 200 bird paintings in his portfolio. Some of his drawings were exhibited in Edinburgh and there he met with the engraver W H Lizars who made several copper plates of his paintings, but was halted in the production by industrial unrest. When Audubon visited London to give a paper at the Royal Society he met with Robert Havel and his son, both excellent engravers and painters. Audubon transferred his project to London and to the Havell workshop where over the next twelve years the engraving, printing and colouring of the magnificent plates were carried out.

JOHN JAMES AUDUBON
Red-shouldered hawk,
Buteo lineatus
Birds of America,
1827–1838
Hand-coloured engraving
985 x 650 mm

Swallow-tailed Hawk.
FALCO FURCATUS, Linn,
Male,
Garter Snake.

OPPOSITE Audubon explains in *Ornithological Biography* that this bird feeds on the wing: 'They sweep close over the fields, somtimes seeming to alight for a moment to secure a snake, and holding it fast by the neck, carry it off, and devour it in the air.'

ABOVE In the text accompanying this image of the armadillo it is described as being like a small pig saddled with the shell of a turtle.

JOHN JAMES AUDUBON
Swallow-tailed kite,
Elanoides forficatus
Birds of America,
1827–1838
Hand-coloured engraving
985 x 650 mm

JOHN JAMES AUDUBON
Nine-banded armadillo,
Dasypus novemcinctus
*The Viviparous Quadrupeds
of North America*, 1848
Hand-coloured lithograph
530 x 690 mm

LEFT As John James Audubon declined into poor health his son, John Woodhouse, took up the task of producing the watercolours for the plates for the work on North American mammals. The plate of the Polar bear is an example of John Woodhouse Audubon's work. The original drawing was made from a specimen in the Charleston Museum as neither father nor son saw a living bear. The text accompanying the plate explains that Audubon visited Labrador in 1833 in search of the polar bear but was unsuccessful, 'it being midsummer'.

JOHN JAMES AUDUBON
Polar bear, *Ursus maritimus*
The Viviparous Quadrupeds of North America, 1846
Hand-coloured lithograph
530 x 690 mm

RIGHT This *Physalia* is one of five drawings of the genus by Parkinson, only two of which are finished watercolours, the remaining three being in various stages of completion. Parkinson made the drawings early in the voyage. According to the journal of Joseph Banks, on 7 October 1768 when the morning was calm he 'went out in the boat and took what is calld by the Seamen a Portugese man of war'. The scientist Daniel Solander noted that on 22 and 23 December of the same year, two of these species were collected in the Atlantic Ocean. Parkinson would have made the drawing very soon after collection as both Solander and Joseph Banks closely studied the *Physalia*, which included dissecting the species.

SYDNEY PARKINSON
Portuguese man of war,
Physalia physalis
Watercolour, 1768
370 x 270 mm

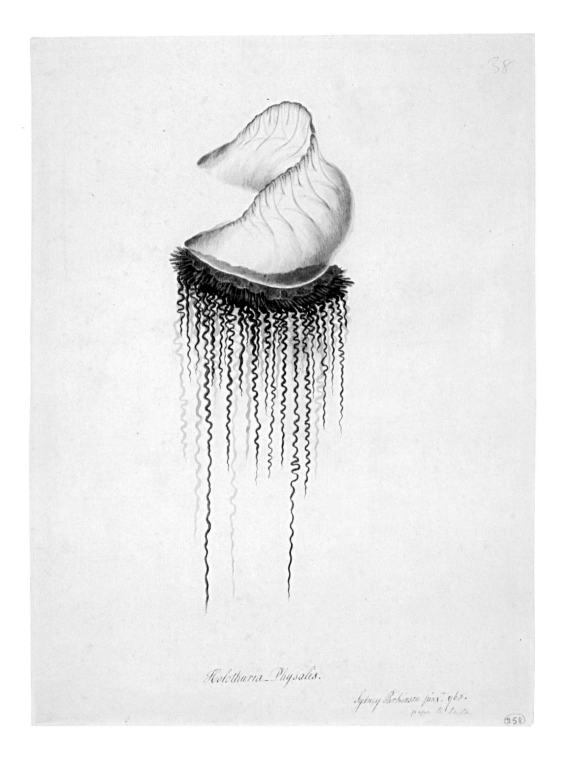

Holothuria Physalis.

Sydney Parkinson pinxt. 768.

Galyxis ternaria.

Sydney Parkinson pinx. 1768.

Brasil

LEFT This South American climbing plant was named for the French navigator, Admiral Louis Antoine de Bougainville, who collected the plant on his return voyage around the world in 1768. That same year James Cook set sail on his three-year circumnavigation of the world, and when the *Endeavour* landed in Brazil, Sydney Parkinson completed this watercolour of the plant.

SYDNEY PARKINSON
Bougainvillea, *Bougainvillea spectabilis*
Watercolour, 1768
470 x 280 mm

RIGHT In December 1774, the *Resolution* entered the cold and inhospitable waters of Tierra del Fuego where the crew celebrated the Christmas festival over several days. On Christmas morning, Forster was amongst a group of men who went to collect geese for the celebratory meal, capturing no fewer than 53 birds. Forster painted a number of species of bird during this month including this raptor, the southern caracara, which he painted on the 26 December whilst most of the crew were becoming intoxicated.

GEORG FORSTER
Crested caracara,
Polyborus plancus
Watercolour, [1774]
540 x 360 mm

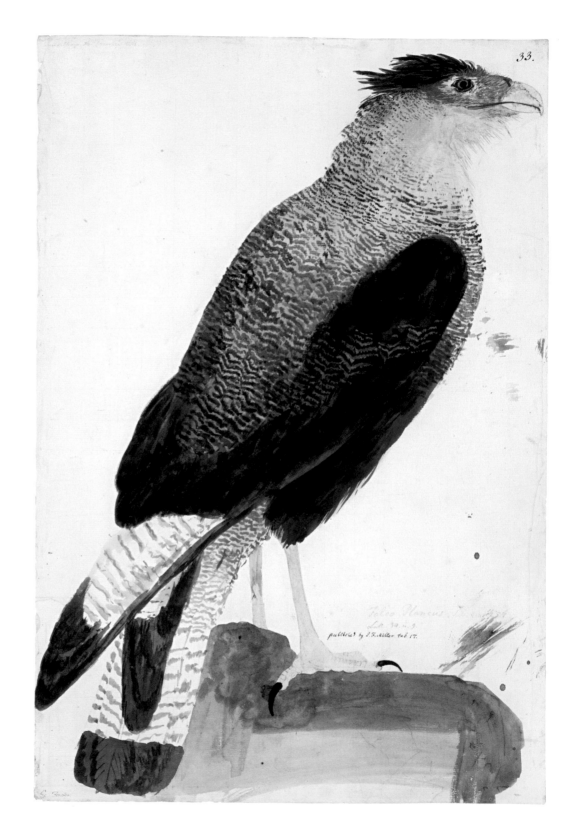

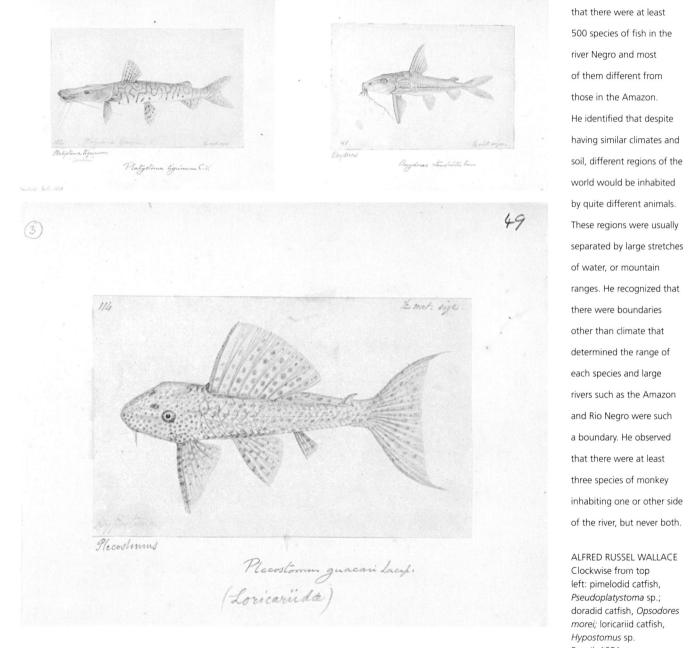

Platystoma tigrinum C.V.

Onydoras steudachteri lower

Plecostomus

Plecostomus guacari Lacep.

(Loricariidæ)

LEFT Wallace estimated that there were at least 500 species of fish in the river Negro and most of them different from those in the Amazon. He identified that despite having similar climates and soil, different regions of the world would be inhabited by quite different animals. These regions were usually separated by large stretches of water, or mountain ranges. He recognized that there were boundaries other than climate that determined the range of each species and large rivers such as the Amazon and Rio Negro were such a boundary. He observed that there were at least three species of monkey inhabiting one or other side of the river, but never both.

ALFRED RUSSEL WALLACE
Clockwise from top left: pimelodid catfish, *Pseudoplatystoma* sp.; doradid catfish, *Opsodores morei;* loricariid catfish, *Hypostomus* sp.
Pencil, 1851
100 x 160 mm

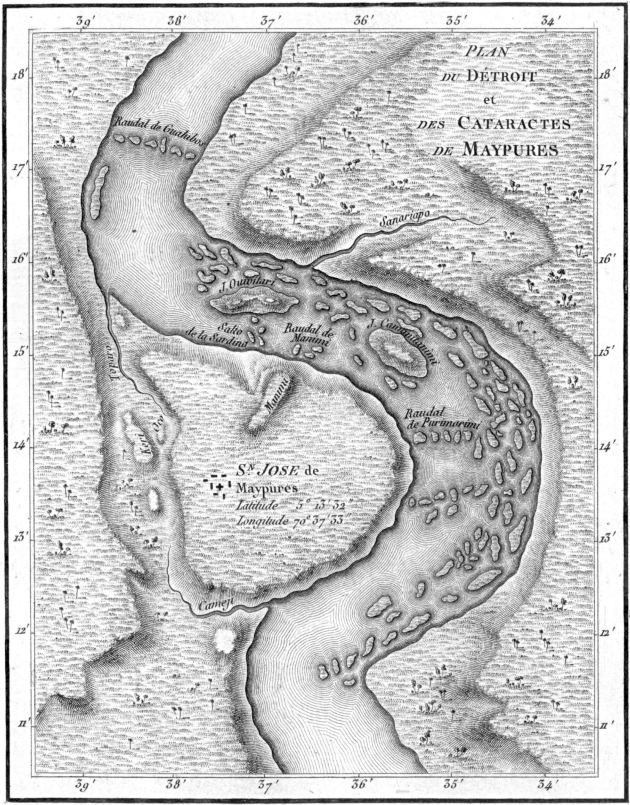

PLAN
DU DÉTROIT
et
DES CATARACTES
DE MAYPURES

Sanariapo

Raudal de Guahibos

J. Ouivitari

Salto de la Sardina

Raudal de Manini

J. Carnanianimi

Raudal de Purunarimi

Toparo

Keri Oro

Manini

S.ᴺ JOSE de Maypures
Latitude   5° 13' 32"
Longitude 70° 37' 33"

Cameji

Dessiné par Alex. de Humboldt en Avril 1800.

Simia melanocephala.

OPPOSITE Alexander Humboldt made many maps throughout his travels in South America. This map of the Cataracts of Maypures was completed in April 1800. In his book *Personal Narrative* Humboldt explains that there were two great cataracts on the Orinoco river, one of which is Maypures. Humboldt and Bonpland had an unnerving experience here when they believed they were stranded in a cavern behind the waterfall, as 'night and a furious storm approached'. Fortunately they were rescued after several hours.

LEFT Humboldt acquired a large zoological collection during his travels, including seven parrots, a toucan and other birds, a dog and nine monkeys. He purchased this uakari while on the Casiguiare canal. Humboldt provided extensive knowledge of New World fauna to the scientific world, writing essays on electric eels, piranhas, salamanders and the monkeys of the forests of South America.

ALEXANDER HUMBOLDT
Plan du Detroit et des
Cataractes de Maypures
*Atlas Géographique et
Physique du Nouveau
Continent*, 1814.
Engraving
147 x 113 mm

ALEXANDER HUMBOLDT
Black uakari, *Cacajao
melanocephalus*
*Recueil d'observations de
zoologie et d'anatomie
comparâee*, 1812
Hand-coloured engraving
336 x 255 mm

This is the view of Mount Chimborazo before Humboldt
and Bonpland set out to climb it. At 6,279 m (20,600 ft)
Chimborazo was believed to be the highest mountain in the
world at that time and Humboldt's ascent to within 396 m
(1300 ft) of the summit was recognized as a magnificent
achievement. It was more than 30 years before Humboldt's
mountaineering altitude record was broken.

ALEXANDER HUMBOLDT
Le Chimborazo vu Depuis le
Plateau de Tapia
Vues des Cordillères, 1810
Hand-coloured engraving
572 x 790 mm

Rochers basaltiques et Cascade de Regla.

OPPOSITE This engraving is of the famous landform that spans a very deep canyon in which flows the Rio de la Sama Paz. This river, Humboldt explained, was almost inaccessible and 'could not have been crossed without extreme difficulty had not nature provided two bridges of rocks'. Humboldt claimed, 'amidst the majestic and varied scenery of the Cordilleras, the vallies most powerfully affect the imagination of the European traveller… I doubt whether in any part of the Globe a phenomenon has been discovered so extraordinary as that of the three masses of rocks, which support each other by forming a natural arch'.

LEFT This basalt rock formation lay near the Real del Monte silver mine in northeast Mexico. The basalt columns, Humboldt observed, were similar to the Giant's Causeway in Antrim, Northern Ireland, and the columns in the volcanic region of the Vivarais in France. Humboldt saw this as evidence of the same geological process taking place under different climates, in different parts of the world and at very different epochs in time. He stated that: 'In every place the same appearances attest the same order in the revolutions, which have progressively changed the surface of the Globe.'

ALEXANDER HUMBOLDT
Ponts Naturels d'Icononzo
Vues des Cordillères, 1810
Engraving
564 x 400 mm

ALEXANDER HUMBOLDT
Rochers Basaltiques et
Cascade de Regla
Vues des Cordillères, 1810
572 x 400 mm

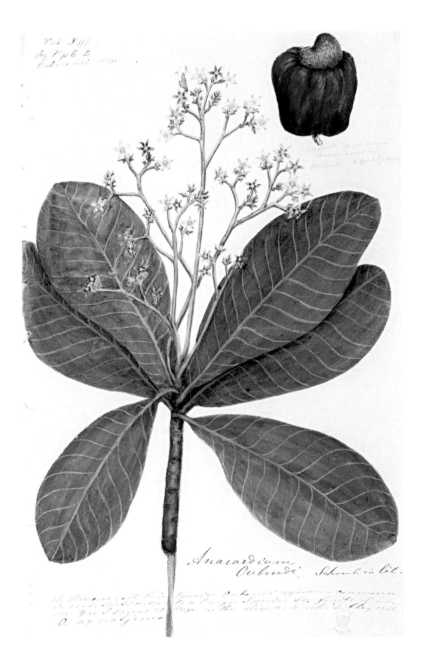

LEFT The cashew is native to northeastern Brazil. The local name given to this plant is tupi, which gave rise to the Portuguese name caju from which cashew is derived.

ROBERT SCHOMBURGK
Cashew, *Anacardium occidentale*
Watercolour, 1840s
330 x 205 mm

OPPOSITE The Malabar or Guyana chestnut is a large flowering tree. It is found along estuaries and lakeshores in the tropical rainforests of Mexico, Central and South America. The beautiful flowers are particularly fragrant in the evening and the edible seed are contained in long brown pods, some as long as 30 cm.

ROBERT SCHOMBURGK
Malabar or Guyana chestnut, *Pachira aquatica*
Watercolour, 1840s
263 x 205 mm

Carolinea

Pach. aequatica Aublet.

RIGHT AND OPPOSITE

These two illustrations are recto and verso of a single sheet. Schomburgk was clearly experimenting on how best to depict this plant providing both a traditional view (right) as well as one where the white flowers are set against a black background (opposite).

ROBERT SCHOMBURGK
Orchid
Watercolour, c.1840s
361 x 261 mm

Australa

ELLIS **MARTENS** GOULD **COOK** WATLING **PARKINSON** WEBBER **BAUER** FC

sia

AUSTRALASIA:
Land of the Dreaming and Penal Colony

SCOTTISH ARTIST SYDNEY PARKINSON was the first European to produce natural history drawings of Australian flora and fauna. He was employed by Joseph Banks as an artist on James Cook's famous *Endeavour* voyage (1768–1771). Cook's initial mission was to sail to Tahiti to observe the 1769 transit of Venus across the face of the Sun. But with this undertaking completed, Cook 'was to carry into execution the Additional Instructions contained in the inclosed Sealed Packet'.[1] The instructions were for him to sail south to find the undiscovered land mass known as *Terra Australis Incognito* and 'observe the Nature of the Soil, and the products thereof'. Specimens of any 'Mines, Minerals or valuable stones' that were found were to be brought back to Britain, and observations of the 'Genius, Temper, Disposition and Number of the Natives…'[2] were also to be made.

That natural history should have played such a major role on the voyage was down to the persuasive powers of Joseph Banks. He convinced the Admiralty that a survey of the natural history of any land they encountered, together with drawings, specimens and descriptions of what they found on the voyage, was essential to the expedition's success. One month before Cook was to sail he was informed that a further nine civilians were to be accommodated on his very small ship. It was said that 'No people ever went to sea better fitted out for the purpose of Natural History'[3] and, led by Banks, the party also included Daniel Solander, a scientist who had trained under Carl Linnaeus, the artist Alexander Buchan and Herman Diedrich Spöring, who acted as secretary as well as being a skilled artist. A second appointed artist was the 24-year-old Sydney Parkinson from Edinburgh in Scotland.

Parkinson came from a poor Quaker family and his father died when he was five years of age. He grew up to be a shy, innocent young man of slender build and, on completion of his schooling, he was apprenticed to a woollen draper. His talent as an artist was evident from an early age and when his family moved to London he came to the attention of the nurseryman James Lee, who introduced him to Joseph Banks. Parkinson soon impressed Banks with his skilled botanical artistry and he was invited to join the *Endeavour* voyage as a natural history artist. For Parkinson this was the opportunity of a lifetime, a chance to establish a future career as a specialist artist.

By the time the *Endeavour* had left the shores of South America in 1769, Parkinson had already completed over 150 paintings. When the ship arrived in New Zealand and Australia, he found that time was against him. The abundance of new flora and fauna of these lands was so great that Parkinson was forced to alter his work pattern. Without the time to complete many of his drawings he now made sketches, adding in the key colours with the intention of completing them when he came home to Britain. Joseph Banks fully intended having the botanical drawings published, so working up the sketches to finished watercolours ready for engraving would keep Parkinson employed for some considerable time.

For two full years Parkinson worked assiduously on sketching and drawing the plants, animals, birds and fish of the South Pacific. His work was developing well and the future looked bright when tragedy struck. The *Endeavour* was making its return home across the Atlantic when it put in for repairs at Batavia. It was here that Parkinson and three members of the crew were struck down with dysentery and malaria. Parkinson died on 26th January 1771 and was buried at sea, some five months' travel from the shores of England.

Life on board the *Endeavour* was hard. Conditions in the cabins were cramped, unhealthy and claustrophobic, whilst working on deck was impossible. The food was certainly not up to the standard Banks was used to and the climatic conditions on land were insufferable at times. Despite all this, Banks still wished to accompany Cook on his second voyage in HMS *Resolution* in 1772. The Admiralty turned down his request and appointed the naturalist Johann Forster, accompanied by his 17-year-old son, Georg, as assistant naturalist and artist. The Forsters were of German origin and fully immersed in the intellectual ethos of the time. They were directly appointed by the Admiralty for this voyage and considered themselves professional naturalists. Johann Forster was one of the earliest advocates for such a profession and defined the role through his own practice on board the *Resolution* by being disciplined in his systematic recordings and descriptions of species collected and drawn on the voyage. Both the elder and younger Forster wrote of their travels once they had returned; their work reflecting their interest in the relationship between climate, vegetation and human development. Their views influenced many natural scientists of the time, including Banks and Alexander Humboldt, and helped channel the direction science took in the nineteenth century, with the birth of subjects such as anthropology and ethnography.

SYDNEY PARKINSON
Blue-lined goatfish,
Upeneichthys lineatus
Watercolour, c.1769
269 x 367 mm

The principal purpose of Captain Cook's third voyage was to discover the Northwest Passage between the continents of Asia and America. The route took the expedition via Cape Town and then across the southern part of the Indian Ocean to Tasmania, New Zealand and Tahiti. From there Cook sailed north on to the Bering Strait. In late 1778 he returned to Hawaii for the winter and it was there, on 14th February 1779, that he was killed. The official artist on the voyage was John Webber who sailed on the *Resolution*. Webber produced a large number of watercolour landscapes, ethnographic drawings, particularly of Hawaiians, and some natural history illustrations. On board the *Discovery* was William Ellis, surgeon's mate and artist. Ellis produced a collection of watercolour drawings and sketches of natural history subjects, predominantly of birds. His draughtsmanship was by no means comparable with the accomplished work of Webber, but Ellis managed to document several species unknown to science at the time.

The next stage in Australia's natural history art also owed much to Joseph Banks. He had returned from Cook's first voyage a popular hero and a man of repute amongst the learned community. He was elected president of the Royal Society in 1778 and was now in a position where

RIGHT This map of the southern hemisphere is one of several made by James Cook from the *Resolution* voyage of 1772–1775, which he published in his journal of the voyage to the South Pole.

JAMES COOK
Chart of the Southern Hemisphere
A Voyage Towards the South Pole and Round the World,
1777
Engraving
553 x 547 mm

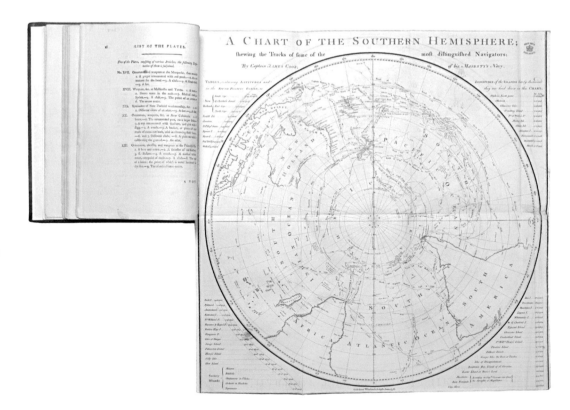

he could influence some of the key decision makers in government and commerce. His authority increased as the century came to a close and very little happened in the area of natural history that did not have some link to Banks. Whether it was direct funding, selecting personnel for expeditions, persuading government agents and arms of the state in policy or even just voicing his opinion, Banks was ever present.

In the mid-1780s it was Joseph Banks who suggested using Botany Bay in Australia as a suitable location for some of the inmates of Britain's overcrowded prisons. After the American Revolution it was no longer possible to deport the unwanted layers of the British criminal classes to the shores of Georgia in America and an alternative destination was required. The Admiralty had already seen the need for a naval supply base in Australia and what better way to build it than with the free labour provided by convicts. Banks' proposal was accepted and on 13th May 1787, eleven ships set sail from Portsmouth, England, bound for Port Jackson, present day Sydney. Known as the First Fleet these ships were laden with convicts who would serve their punishment in an alien and unforgiving environment with a hostile and relentless climate. Alongside the convicts were government officials, crew members and marines with their wives and families. In total just under 1,400 people arrived in Port Jackson, but there were no official naturalists or artists amongst them. No thought was given by the Admiralty of including either profession on the First Fleet, and it was a further 13 years before the arrival of Ferdinand Bauer and Robert Brown, who were sponsored by the British authorities to carry out such professional work.

It was left to a few convicts and some officers schooled in the naval tradition of draughtsmanship of coastal profiles and chart making to produce the artwork from the first decade of European settlement in Australia. One of the officers was the midshipman of HMS *Sirius*, George Raper, who was born in London in 1769. Raper completed a large number of drawings during his five year assignment to the Antipodes and his contribution to the body of work for this period of Australian art is not insignificant. His draughtsmanship is proficient and although the focus is flora and fauna, his more interesting drawings tend to be topographical depictions of Port Jackson and its close environs. Raper's own interest in the plants and animals of this new land is apparent, but also evident is his lack of scientific knowledge of the subject that was such a crucial element for botanical

ABOVE This cabbage is native to Kerguelen island which lies midway between Africa and Australia. Cook landed there during his third voyage, and referred to it as Desolation Island. Little seemed to grow there but moss and this member of the cabbage family.

JOHN WEBBER
Kerguelen Island cabbage,
Pringlea antiscorbutica
Watercolour and bodycolour,
c.1777
222 x 188 mm

artists such as Parkinson and the Austrian-born Ferdinand Bauer. Like all artists of the first decade of settlement, Raper lacked both the skill of a professional and, having no experienced naturalist to refer to, the detailed accuracy required for scientific illustration.

As Raper set sail from Australia to return to Britain in 1791, the third contingent of convicts was being transported across the southern seas to Botany Bay. On board was Thomas Watling, who had been accused of forging 'Guinea notes' and offered himself for transportation rather than risk the hanging that could follow a trial. He was given a 14-year sentence to be served in Australia. Watling was of Scottish origin, born in Dumfries where he was raised by his aunt as both of his parents had died when he was an infant. He was relatively well educated, particularly in art, and for a time ran his own art academy. Watling managed to abscond when in port at Cape Town but was arrested by the Dutch and sent on to New South Wales to serve his sentence. At Port Jackson he was promptly assigned to the surgeon general of the colony, John White, who was a keen amateur naturalist and it was under his instruction that Watling made his drawings. Watling was an unwilling artist for White and he resented his treatment by him and other officers, although time spent drawing was a preferable occupation to that of hewing stones or felling trees. White objected to Watling signing his drawings but, despite this, a fair number carry Watling's signature. Whether these formed part of White's collection or remained in Watling's possession as part of those that he intended to have published once his freedom was obtained is unknown. Watling, like most of the early artists in Australia, produced drawings in watercolour, washes, ink and pencil and focused on the flora, fauna and landscapes of the region. He also produced a set of pencil sketches of the Eora people, the name given to Aborigines of the coastal area of Sydney.

The first drawings of Aborigines by Europeans vary in quality and accuracy. The so-called objectivity applied to drawing plants and animals is not possible when recording people with whom the artist cannot help but interact. All are tainted by the artists' preconceived ideas of the indigenous societies they encountered and some portraits such as those by Richard Browne are little more than caricatures. For Watling, and the unknown artist who has been given the generic name of Port Jackson Painter, efforts to depict Aboriginal lifestyle and artefacts were an attempt to record and document what they observed. Watling's sketches of known individuals certainly convey a more sympathetic approach to the subject despite his disdain for them, as revealed in his letters to his aunt. Watling served less than his 14 years' sentence having been granted a conditional pardon in 1797. He returned to Dumfries where, despite attempts to make a living as 'the Limner in the Town',[4] he was never very successful and was reduced to appealing to members of the Admiralty for support in his later life.

A Native Wounded while asleep

The first professional artists sponsored by governments arrived in Australia in 1801 with the French and British expeditions under Nicolas Baudin and Matthew Flinders, respectively. Both captains had been given instructions to chart the coastline of Australia and both had naturalists and artists on board their ships. Baudin had two ships under his command, *Naturaliste* and *Geographe*, and his party included the natural history artist Charles Lesueur and anthropologist Nicolas Petit. Baudin's ships arrived in Australia in May 1801. Flinders commanded HMS *Investigator* and arrived in Australia in the December of the same year. The expeditions circumnavigated the Australian continent in opposite directions and in April 1802 they met at Encounter Bay, named by Flinders after the event. Flinders had on board with him the naturalist Robert Brown, the landscape artist William Westall and natural history artist Ferdinand Bauer. The British Admiralty had appointed all three. Landscape artists had always been recognized as important as their work was sometimes crucial for navigation and chart making. Natural history artists were not so valued, although Bauer was paid considerably more than the scientist Robert Brown. The commitment by the Admiralty to support the natural history element of Flinders' voyage was accomplished only after intense lobbying from Sir Joseph Banks. He persuaded the head of the Admiralty of the importance of a natural history survey of the Australian coastline

and his argument was helped by a comparison with the preparations taking place in France for the expedition under Baudin who had a total of 22 scientists, gardeners and artists on board his ships. Even with the Admiralty's support Banks still had to find additional funding to pay for the position of Ferdinand Bauer on the voyage. This he managed to do with a gift of £1,200 from the East India Company which was in exchange for plants that could potentially be grown in the Company's gardens in India and elsewhere.

      Ferdinand Bauer was born in Feldsberg, Austria, now Valtice in the Czech Republic. He was the son of the court painter to the Prince of Lichtenstein but hardly knew his father who died when Ferdinand was two years old. As children Ferdinand and his brothers were given lessons in plant collecting, pressing and drawing and he and two brothers grew up to earn their living as painters. His older brother, Franz, was appointed the first botanical artist at Kew Gardens in England with a salary of £300 a year. Ferdinand, the youngest son of the family, sought his living as artist to scientists and wealthy patrons. He and Franz are recognized today as two of the finest botanical artists of all time. Johann Wolfgang Goethe was enchanted with Ferdinand's work and described it as 'nature is revealed, art concealed, great in its precision, gentle in its execution'.[5]

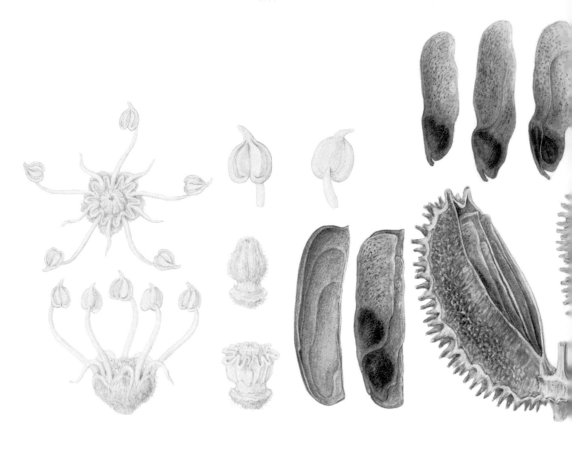

Bauer's drawings from the voyage are exquisite masterpieces of scientific delineation. He possessed a good understanding of plant anatomy and physiology, and he had the help of the brilliant botanist Robert Brown who worked alongside him on the voyage. For two years the *Investigator* travelled the coastline of Australia and while Flinders took readings and made charts, Bauer and Brown would head off further into the interior of Australia, collecting, sketching and making notes. Bauer's boyhood tutor had shown him how to use a colour-coded chart with over 140 shades. By the time Bauer travelled to Australia he had expanded this chart to over 300 shades. This enabled him to make sketches on which he placed numbers for the appropriate colour, which he would later work up in more comfortable and time-permitting circumstances. It took on average a week's work to complete a single finished watercolour.

The difficulties in surveying and collecting specimens in unknown and often dangerous terrain were made worse by the relentless and tyrannical summer heat that took its toll on each and every one on board ship. Almost every member of the crew, including Flinders, Brown and Bauer, succumbed to bouts of scurvy, dysentery or sunstroke. Added to this was the continuous effort to maintain the ship, which had never been in good condition even from the start of the voyage and, by the end of 1802, hardly had a 'sound timber in her'.[6] By June 1803 the *Investigator* was leaking so

badly that it was considered beyond repair. Flinders made the decision to return to England to collect another ship to complete his survey and bring home those crew members left in Port Jackson. Fortune, however, did not favour Flinders and one catastrophe followed another. Seven days after leaving Port Jackson, his ship HMS *Porpoise* struck a reef and Flinders had to make the hazardous journey back to Port Jackson in a small boat. He then took command of the *Cumberland* which also proved to be in such a poor condition that he was forced to dock in Mauritius, which was under French rule. Unknown to Flinders the war between Britain and Napoleonic France had recommenced in the May of that year and Flinders soon found himself under arrest. He spent six-and-a-half years as a prisoner in Mauritius and when he returned to England in 1810 he never truly recovered from the ordeal.

Ferdinand Bauer and the botanist Robert Brown remained in Australia for a further two years, working on the natural history of New South Wales. They also made separate expeditions further afield, Brown to Tasmania and Bauer to Norfolk Island, which had been colonized in 1788 and, like New South Wales, had become a penal settlement. Bauer and Brown returned to England in 1805 but no welcoming party was organized to meet them, such as the one Humboldt received in Paris the year before. Banks did all he could to win support from the Admiralty for the two to complete their work on identifying, classifying and drawing the many specimens they had brought back with them.

ABOVE The botanist Robert Brown named this tree for Matthew Flinders, the captain of the *Investigator* on which he and the artist Bauer sailed. The sketches for the drawing were made at Broad Sound, Queensland in September 1802, where they found the tree 'in flower and with ripe capsules'.

FERDINAND BAUER
Crow's ash, *Flindersia australis*,
Watercolour, 1802
520 x 353 mm

However, the same public who had lionized Cook after his voyages to Australia now had new heroes such as Admiral Nelson.

During the first 50 years of white settlement in Australia, artwork depicting the land, its natural history and people was made for the European market, to be sold and reproduced in magazines and books. By the 1830s there were still very few resident artists in Australia and much was learnt about the country through the output of visiting artists and naturalists. One such visitor was John Gould who, with his wife Elizabeth and their son Henry, spent two years from 1838 travelling through Australia collecting and drawing birds. Before leaving for Australia, Gould had embarked on a project to produce a work on Australian birds. Returning from their travels the couple were equipped to transform those early ideas and their efforts resulted in their magnificent seven-volume work, *The Birds of Australia*.

It was only with the growing number of professional artists settling permanently in the colony that the approach to depicting Australian fauna and flora began to change. Few of these artists found they could survive through their art alone and most took up other professions. One who managed to eke out a meagre living for many years as an artist was Conrad Martens. Martens was born in London in 1801 and as a teenager decided to make a career as an artist with a particular interest in landscape drawing. He remained a struggling artist up to the age of 32 when, with a determination to transform his fortune, he set sail for South America. Hearing of a ship's captain looking for an artist, Martens made himself known and was recruited by Captain FitzRoy of HMS *Beagle*. The *Beagle* was docked in Montevideo at the time and had left England two years previously with the artist Augustus Earle on board. But Earle's health was failing and he resigned his post to return to England. The *Beagle* left Montevideo on 6th December 1833 with Martens as the artist.

He was soon not only producing drawings for FitzRoy but also giving lessons to several of the sailors, one of whom was Syms Covington, the young man assigned to Charles Darwin as his assistant. Martens remained with the *Beagle* for a year producing a fair body of work and becoming a friend and companion to Darwin.

In 1835 Martens travelled to Australia and settled in Sydney where he established himself as a landscape artist, painting mostly in watercolour. In later years he travelled to some of the frontier towns such as Brisbane to sketch and prepare his watercolours of the area. He eventually completed over 70 watercolours on commission, many of which have survived. Martens lived out his life in Australia and died in 1878. Much of his work is now in Australian museums and galleries and he is recognized as one of the pioneering professional artists of Australia.

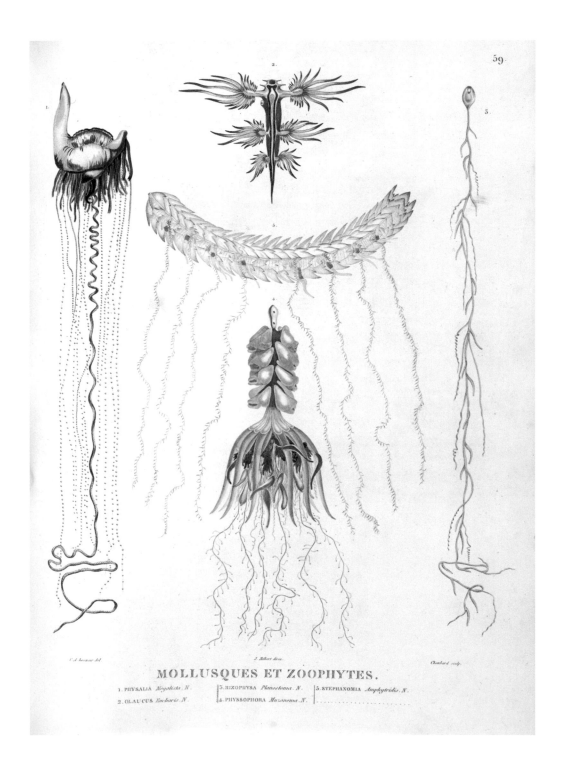

MOLLUSQUES ET ZOOPHYTES.

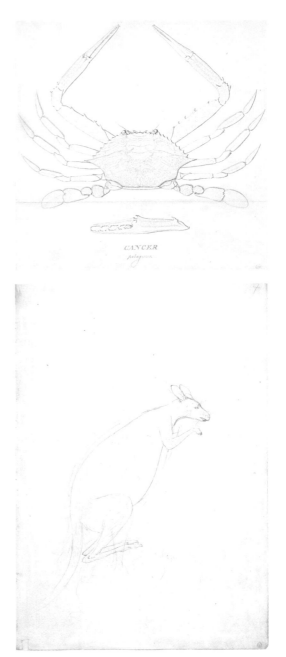

OPPOSITE Sydney Parkinson never completed full watercolour drawings of his sketches of Australian plants; instead these were made by one of five artists Joseph Banks employed when he returned to England. The majority of these watercolours were produced by Frederick Nodder, who in addition to having Parkinson's sketch would also refer to a specimen, the descriptive notes made by Banks or Solander at the time of the sketch, and occasionally a living plant.

SYDNEY PARKINSON
Red passion flower, *Passiflora aurantia*
Sketch pencil and watercolour, c.1770
539 x 373 mm
Finished watercolour, 1780
541 x 373 mm

RIGHT The top pencil sketch is one of the few drawings from the *Endeavour* voyage not by Sydney Parkinson. The artist was the Swedish-born Herman Diedrich Spöring, assistant to Daniel Solander. His role was to transcribe Solander and Banks' scientific notes as fair copies. Spöring died two days before Parkinson on the homeward journey in January 1771. The sketch below is one of the first known European drawings of a kangaroo. Parkinson drew it in June 1770, when the *Endeavour* was undergoing repairs on the Endeavour River near what is now Cooktown, Queensland. On the verso is written 'Kanguru' in Joseph Banks' hand.

HERMAN DIEDRICH SPÖRING
Blue crab, *Portunus pelagicus*
Pencil, c.1769
376 x 372 mm

SYDNEY PARKINSON
Kangaroo
Pencil, [1770]
525 x 358 mm

LEFT Cook's second voyage did not go to Australia, although the *Resolution*'s sister ship the *Adventure* landed in Van Dieman's Land, present day Tasmania. It had been agreed that the two ships should rendezvous at Queen Charlotte's Sound, New Zealand and it was here and also at Dusky Bay that Forster spent time collecting and painting the flora and fauna of the country. It was at Dusky Bay that Forster made this drawing of Pimelea.

OPPOSITE Entering the Southern Ocean in early December 1772, Forster noted that they saw penguins for the first time on the voyage and these were closely followed by their first sightings of icebergs. It was also in these latitudes that they saw the phenomena known as the southern lights, *Aurora Australis.* Georg Forster produced paintings of six different species of penguin over the course of the voyage. Johann Forster was the first to describe *Pygoscelis antarcticus* when his work was published in 1781.

GEORG FORSTER
Pimelea gnidia
Watercolour and ink, 1773
481 x 327 mm

GEORG FORSTER
Chinstrap penguin,
Pygoscelis antarcticus
Watercolour, c.1773
481 x 341 mm

82

about 2/3 natural size

G. Forster

Aptenodytes antarctica J.R.Forster in Commentat. Götting. 3.p.141 tab.4.
J.G.XVII:557-4.   his figure.

aptenodytes antarctica

ABOVE Cook visited the Kingdom of Tonga on his second voyage, calling them the friendly islands. On the third voyage the duration of his stay in the islands lasted the whole month of July, allowing Anderson and Ellis to collect specimens and make fairly extensive observations. The fruit bat or flying fox depicted in this drawing is relatively common on many of the islands of Tonga. They live in large colonies and are known to migrate between islands.

WILLIAM ELLIS
Flying fox, *Pteropus* sp.
Watercolour, c.1777
190 x 286 mm

LEFT On his return from Cook's last voyage William Ellis published his account of the expedition in two volumes. A small number of ethnographic drawings appear in the published work but none of his drawings of plants, animals or birds is included. In 1785 a report in the Gentleman's Magazine, volume 55, described how Ellis had died after falling from a mainmast of a ship at Ostend.

WILLIAM ELLIS
Black-faced cuckoo-shrike,
Coracina novaehollandiae
Watercolour, 1777
245 x 170 mm

Soon after the arrival of the First Fleet at Sydney Cove, Port

Jackson, a second penal settlement was established on Norfolk

Island. In March 1790, two ships, the *Sirius* and *Supply*, sailed

there with 280 people aboard. After the men, women and

children had disembarked and some of the stores unloaded,

Sirius was swept against a reef and wrecked. Raper completed

several drawings of the wreck.

GEORGE RAPER
Norfolk Island and the wreck of the *Sirius*
Watercolour, 1790
337 x 490 mm

ABOVE George Raper was stranded on Norfolk Island for 11 months following the wrecking of the *Sirius* on 19 March 1790. Whilst there, he completed many of his watercolour drawings of topographical scenes, plants and animals, including fish.

GEORGE RAPER
Trumpet emperor fish,
Lethrinus miniatus
Watercolour, 1790
334 x 490 mm

OPPOSITE When first observed, the emu was thought to be an ostrich but as many travellers soon discovered there were several large, flightless birds that inhabited this new land.

GEORGE RAPER
Emu, *Dromaius
novaehollandiae*
Watercolour, 1791
476 x 315 mm

EMU of PORT JACKSON. References -
1 A Body Feather of the Natural Size - 2 The Egg 5 Inches by 3¼ from the only one Yet seen

Scale of Feet)

RIGHT inscribed on the bottom of this drawing is 'Gna.na.gna.na.' This could be the known Aborigine Gnunga Gnunga, brother-in-law to Bennelong and friend of Balloderree,

PORT JACKSON PAINTER
Gna.na.gna.na
Watercolour, c.1788–1797
286 x 207 mm

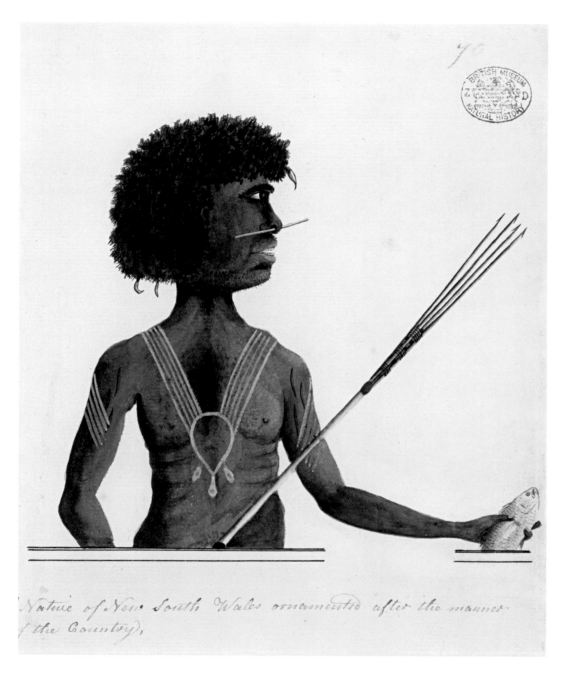

Native of New South Wales ornamented after the manner of the Country.

LEFT Many of the drawings of the Eora people depict body decoration, which included both paint and cicatrices or raised scars. Also displayed are ornaments for the hair and nose as well as necklaces, headbands and waistbands. Many are identified as being made from animal bone or teeth.

PORT JACKSON PAINTER
A Native of New South Wales ornamented after the manner of the Country
Watercolour, c.1788–1797
211 X 177 mm

Great brown Kingfisher: a small variety. Lathams Syn =.
= 2.p.609.
Two thirds the Natural size
Native name Goo-ge-na-gan:

OPPOSITE 'The black Swan, the size of an English Swan Native name Mulgo.' Several of the men from the First Fleet who wrote journals of their stay in Australia reported that they only noticed the white tips of the wings of this bird once it was in flight. Most of the comments about this swan were written in 1788 and it is likely that is when the drawing was completed.

PORT JACKSON PAINTER
Black swan, *Cygnus atratus*
Watercolour, [1788]
243 x 193 mm

LEFT This great brown kingfisher is now known as the laughing kookaburra and is endemic throughout eastern Australia. Inscribed on the drawing is: 'Two thirds the Natural size Native name Goo-ge-na-gan.'

PORT JACKSON PAINTER
Laughing kookaburra,
Dacelo novaeguineae
Watercolour, c.1788–1797
220 x 163 mm

ABOVE An accompanying note explains that 'this drawing is about one half the size of Nature. However in that point they vary exceedingly for they are to be found much larger, and also much smaller..... Like all the Lizards or Guana tribe they live in holes of Rocks, the Earth & c & c and Insects are their food.'

THOMAS WATLING
Monitor lizard, *Varanus* sp.
Watercolour, c.1792–1797
122 x 349 mm

Tho: Watling, delt.

RIGHT AND OPPOSITE

'The Natural size. This is a
rare Bird, only been seen on
some logoons . A species of
the Avocetta. Native name
Antiquatich.' The natural
history drawings and the
accompanying annotations
provide current researchers
with a knowledge of species
observed during early
settlement of the region.

PORT JACKSON PAINTER
Red-necked avocet,
*Recurvirostra
novaehollandiae*
Watercolour, 1788–1797
470 x 265 mm

PORT JACKSON PAINTER
Red-necked avocet,
*Recurvirostra
novaehollandiae*
Watercolour, 1788–1797
203 x 146 mm

American Avoset. Syn 5. 295

263.

22 Inches from the extremities. This Bird is found along the shores of the sea coast. American Avoset Latham Syn 5. p. 295. Pl. 92

366

RIGHT 'This small tree grows to about the height of eight or ten feet…The Native name Warratta'. Watling was assigned to John White, the Surgeon General of the First Fleet, who took a very keen interest in the natural history of Australia. In 1790 White published his Journal of a voyage to New South Wales, which included 65 coloured plates of plants, animals, birds and other natural productions. The illustrations were made by several artists and it is thought Watling was influenced by their manner and style in his depiction of wildlife.

THOMAS WATLING
Waratah, *Telopea speciossima*.
Watercolour, 1792–1797
366 x 218 mm

Thomas Watling. delt.

This small tree grows to about the height of eight or ten feet; its leaves stringing out alternately above each other, in this manner, ℞ — When the flower falls the pods appear as underneath, sometimes to the number of six, (but not as represented open,) from whence succeeding branches shoot and flourish as the former. The Native name Warratta

LEFT Each of these drawings has detailed notes attached describing appearance, habitat and information gleaned from the local Eora people. For the echidna these were: 'Native Name Burroo-gin- The Natives informed me this Animal (which is very shy and can conceal itself in the Earth by scratching a Hole with the greatest readiness & rapidity) tho' rarely seen by us is pretty numerous in the interior parts of the Country; they added that the flesh they consider a great delicacy.'

THOMAS WATLING
Echidna,
Tachyglossus aculeatus
Watercolour, 1792–1797
149 x 296 mm

THOMAS WATLING
Leaf-tailed gecko,
Phyllurus platurus
Watercolour, 1792–1797
120 x 230 mm

THOMAS WATLING
Bearded dragon,
Pogona barbata
Watercolour, 1792–1797
175 x 296 mm

OPPOSITE This striking portrait of Balloderree includes the distinct markings painted on his body, which had individual significance for him and conveyed meaning to others about himself and his clan.

PORT JACKSON PAINTER
Balloderree
Watercolour, 1788–1797
285 x 210 mm

RIGHT An account of this method of climbing trees was published in *Complete Account of the Settlement at Port Jackson* by Watkin Tench, a British marine officer who sailed with the First Fleet.

PORT JACKSON PAINTER
'Method of climbing trees'
Watercolour, 1788–1797
315 x 190 mm

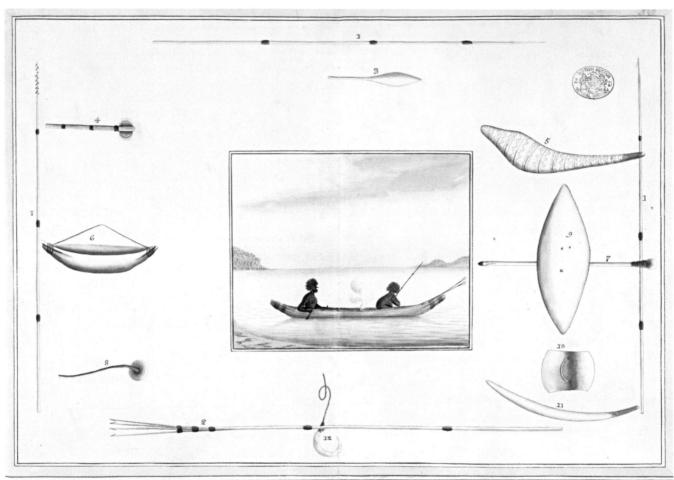

N.º 1 WAR SPEARS. from 10. to 18. Feet.
2 FISH GIG.
3 a PADDLE. 2 Feet.
4 a STONE AXE. handle 2 Feet.
5 a CARVED CLUB. 26 Inches.
6 a VESSEL to Contain Water &c Measuring from 1. to 2 Feet.

N.º 7 THROWING STICK. from 2 to 3 Feet.
8 a PECULIAR CLUB
9 a SHIELD.
10 a SECTION OF THE INSIDE OF A SHIELD. shewing the handle
11 a WOODEN SWORD 3 feet.
12 a FISH HOOK Snooded Middle Size.

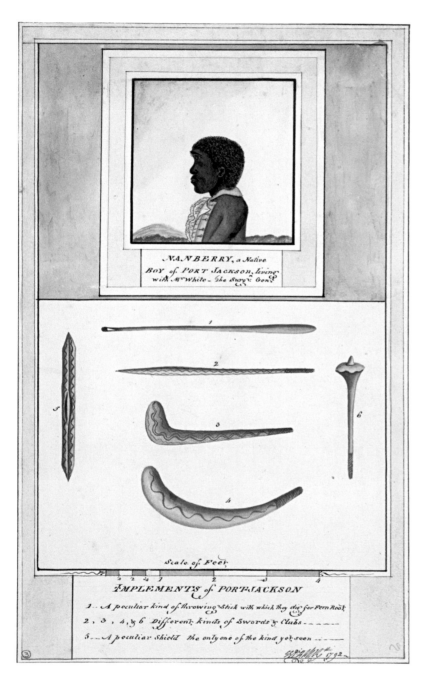

OPPOSITE Ethnographic recordings of the Eora people included portraits, cultural activities such as ceremonies and rituals as well as artefacts considered unusual to Europeans. The implements shown here include a stone axe, a wooden sword, a throwing stick and fish-hooks.

LEFT 'NANBERRY, a Native Boy of PORT JACKSON, living with Mr White – the Surg.-n Gen.-l'. Nanberry went to live with John White at the age of nine or ten. He had been found nursing his father who died of smallpox soon after. His mother and sister had also died of the disease.

GEORGE RAPER
'Natives Fishing in their CANOE. PORT JACKSON'
Watercolour, [1790]
320 x 295 mm

GEORGE RAPER
Nanberry
Watercolour, [1792]
318 x 195 mm

A woman of New south wales cureing the head ache, The blood which she takes from her own gums she supposes comes along the String from the part affected in the patient. This operation they call Bee-an-mee.

ABOVE 'A woman of New South wales cureing the head ache, The blood which she takes from her own gums she supposes comes along the string from the part affected in the patient. This operation they call Bee-an-mee.'

PORT JACKSON PAINTER
'A woman of New south Wales
cureing the head ache'
Watercolour, c.1788–1797
217 x 342 mm

OVERLEAF This unsigned painting is attributed to the 'Port Jackson Painter'. Thomas Watling completed a drawing of the same subject and explained that the local name for this snake was Mal-lea and that it was 'about three feet long'. Many of the drawings are the first illustrations of a species, some of which are rare or have since disappeared.

PORT JACKSON PAINTER
Diamond python,
Morelia spilota
Watercolour, c.1788–1797
318 x 202 mm

RIGHT The destruction of the Aborigine community in and around present day Sydney happened over a very short time period. Within two years of the arrival of the First Fleet over half the population had succumbed to diseases such as smallpox. Within the decade the way of life for the Eora people had almost disappeared. These pencil portraits of known individuals are some of the few existing records of the Eora people that remain.

Clockwise from top left
THOMAS WATLING
COLEBEE
Pencil, c.1792–1797
206 x 112 mm

THOMAS WATLING
NANBREE
Pencil, c.1792–1797
205 x 161 mm

THOMAS WATLING
DA-RING-HA, Cole-bee's
Wife
Pencil, c.1792–1797
205 x 160 mm

THOMAS WATLING
Heads of un-named
Eora Men
Pencil, c.1792–1797
310 x 192 mm

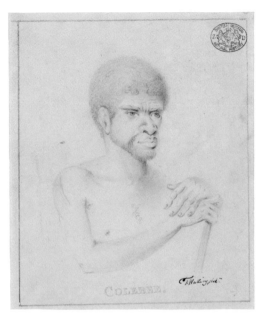

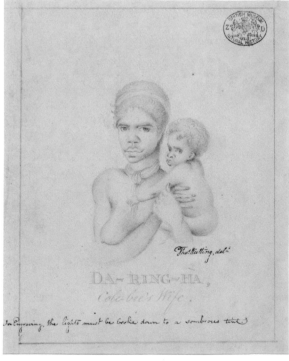

RIGHT *Birds of Australia*,
published by John Gould
in seven volumes from
1840–1848, was one of
the few projects in which
many of the birds were
drawn from nature. The
expeditions and fieldwork
in Tasmania and southern
Australia were long, often
lasting several months at
a time. When travelling in
the less inhabited regions
Gould relied on the expertise
and wildlife knowledge of
the two Aborigines who
travelled with him. Sadly,
Elizabeth Gould died a
year after her return from
Australia and managed to
complete only 84 of the 681
plates. The work is seen as
a valuable contribution to
Australian ornithology.

JOHN GOULD
Satin bowerbird,
Ptilonorhynchus violaceus
Birds of Australia, 1848
Hand-coloured lithograph
540 x 716 mm

PTILONORHYNCHUS HOLOSERICEUS, *Kuhl.*

Colinton from the Woolshed.
C.M. 1860.

LEFT Martens was a landscape rather than a natural history artist, so most of his works are not scientific pieces. In one of his lectures he explained that the purpose of landscape art was to imitate the 'effect which nature has produced'. His experiences whist on the *Beagle* voyage with Charles Darwin would have provided him with an appreciation of the subject of science and knowledge of the importance of observation.

CONRAD MARTENS
Colinton from the woolshed
Pencil and chalk, 1860
320 x 525 mm

Asia

RUSSELL **ROXBURGH** FLEMING **WALLICH** HARDWICKE **HODGSON** SINGH T

RUSSELL **ROXBURGH** FLEMING **WALLICH** HARDWICKE **HODGSON** SINGH

ASIA:
Trade and Empire ~ **India**

THE PRESENCE OF EUROPEANS IN ASIA spans a long period of time and was originally solely commercial. By the eighteenth century both the British and Dutch East India Companies dominated all trade between each of their respective countries and India. A thriving market for things oriental developed in Europe and amongst the most fashionable and wealthy sets it was not unusual to be wearing Indian fabrics or Chinese combs in one's hair, eating and drinking from Chinese porcelain or displaying to friends one's watercolour prints from the East. Some of the earliest studies of Asian plants by Europeans were those by the Portuguese physician, Garcia de Orta, in Goa in the sixteenth century and by the Dutch East India Company in the late seventeenth century. The publication of *Hortus Malabaricus* in 12 volumes from 1678 to 1703 was the result of almost 30 years' research. It is the work of many botanists, physicians, collectors and artists, both Indian and European, and includes descriptions of the plants, with illustrations and their medicinal properties. The plant names are recorded in Latin, Sanskrit, Arabic and Malayalam.

By the late eighteenth century the British East India Company had extended its activities, developing into not only a commercial institution but also a military and political force. It became an unofficial agent of the British government and the government's control of the Company increased further with the appointment of the first Governor General to India in 1773. One of the main aims of the Company was to work out how best to exploit India's natural products and to this end, with support and encouragement from politicians and important naturalists such as Sir Joseph Banks, it established several botanical gardens where it conducted scientific projects and experiments. Experts were appointed to direct the work of the gardens and the Company sponsored expeditions and surveys throughout its territories. Timber for ship-building was in great demand and by the nineteenth century the Company was managing tree plantations and forests. Plants of medicinal and economic value were sought and grown in the Company's gardens. Food crops, plants for dyes and other commercial plants were identified that could be introduced to other parts of the globe where the British had a presence, whilst the gardens were also used to acclimatize newly introduced plants to India. The work conducted by these botanists and naturalists was not only beneficial to the immediate interests of the Company but contributed to the European body of knowledge of the East and to the subject of natural history as a whole.

One of the first naturalists recruited by the East India Company was a student of Linnaeus, the German-born Johann Koenig. He travelled to India independently and worked first as a naturalist for the Indian prince, the Nawab Arcot, before being employed by the Company in 1778. Koenig became good friends with Patrick Russell who had studied medicine at Edinburgh University and travelled in parts of the Middle East before arriving in India. Russell was a keen herpetologist and commissioned drawings of many of the snakes he studied. He was the first European to distinguish harmless from poisonous snakes in India and he was equally interested in other branches of zoology and botany. In 1786 Russell suggested publishing a book on the plants of the region for use by Company officers, a project that Sir Joseph Banks gave his full support to.

The work on the plants of the Coromandel, in southeast India, was published after Russell had left the Company, under the supervision of a fellow Scott, the naturalist William Roxburgh. Like Russell, Roxburgh studied medicine at Edinburgh University and also botany under John Hope at the Edinburgh Botanic Garden. He succeeded Russell as naturalist for the Madras Government and was then appointed superintendent of the Calcutta Botanical Garden in 1793. This was the Company's first botanical garden, opened in 1789, and was situated in Sibpur, just outside Calcutta.

Roxburgh remained superintendent of the Garden for 20 years and has been called the father of Indian botany. Under his directorship the Garden developed into a leading scientific institution where plant experiments were carried out and Indian flora systematically documented. With the establishment of the botanical garden at the Cape of Good Hope, a regular exchange of plants between India and South Africa took place. Roxburgh also embarked on a programme of visually recording many botanical specimens. He employed a series of Indian artists, trained in Mughal art, to produce watercolour drawings of the plants growing in the garden or those brought back from plant-hunting expeditions and surveys. Indian and Chinese artists had a long tradition of illustrating plants and animals, so Company officers adopted the practice of employing local artists rather than recruiting European ones to the regions. This practice continued through to the demise of the Company.

Supervision of the artists' work varied but most were instructed in western style conventions of depicting plants. The purpose of this instruction was to produce botanical illustrations of a scientific

THOMAS HARDWICKE
COLLECTION [J. Hayes]
*Buccinum Harpa, Mollusca
and Radiata of India*
Watercolour, c.1820
265 x 220 mm

nature with the reproductive parts of the plant often magnified to enable identification. At the Calcutta garden Roxburgh appointed his son, John, as head painter to supervise the Indian artists. As knowledge of Indian natural history advanced, the science was given greater support by the Company and by government. But this was a reciprocal relationship, with the science maintaining a critical role as a facilitator and promoter of Empire. Botanical and geographical surveys and knowledge of agricultural and economic crops provided information to those entrusted with political control of the territories.

In 1817 Nathaniel Wallich took over the post of superintendent of the Calcutta Garden. Born in Copenhagen, Wallich had joined the Danish settlement at Serampore in Bengal soon after qualifying as a surgeon in 1806. Two years later the British, who were at war with Denmark, took control of Serampore and Wallich found himself a prisoner of war. Fortunately, he had made a reputation for himself as a knowledgeable botanist so Roxburgh campaigned for Wallich's release and arranged for him to become his assistant at the Calcutta garden. For 30 years Wallich retained the post of superintendent of the Company garden, but left under a cloud resulting from a bitter and acrimonious struggle that had fermented for many years between himself and a young and talented botanist William Griffith. Despite their rivalry, one of their successes was a plant-hunting expedition resulting in the discovery of the tea plant that grew in Assam. Wallich continued the practice of commissioning local artists to draw the plants discovered on such expeditions. He also gave the Indian artists instructions in copper engraving and when the first lithographic press was introduced into India, his artists were taught the process of lithography.[1]

There were three other Company gardens in India, one in each of the Company's provinces, and they also produced a wealth of botanical illustrations. Most notable were the drawings commissioned by John Forbes Royle who took charge of the Saharunpore garden in 1823.

With the establishment of the Company gardens in India the botanical emphasis was of prime importance; but there were also those employed by the Company whose main interest lay in zoology. One such man was Thomas Hardwicke who, in 1778, entered the military service of the Company at the age of 22. By 1819 he had progressed to the rank of Major General and from 1820 was Commandant of Artillery until his retirement in 1823. Hardwicke's passion for natural history was so intense that John Edward Gray, Keeper of Zoology at the British Museum, claimed that because of it Hardwicke had been threatened with confinement by his son-in-law. Hardwicke appears to have had good relationships with both his son-in-laws, making them the main beneficiaries of his will, so the accuracy of Gray's tale is unknown. These two son-in-laws were the husbands of the only known surviving daughters of Hardwicke's five illegitimate children. Hardwicke himself never married. During his time in India and the subcontinent Hardwicke amassed a large and splendid collection of natural history specimens and continued to collect on his retirement in London. His bequest to the British Museum included his books, drawings – which amounted to more than 59 volumes – collections of quadrupeds, skins, zoological specimens in spirits, and cabinets of minerals, rocks, fossils and shells. The largest part of his collection was of birds from around the world and these formed part of his 'Museum room' at his house in Lambeth. Before his death in 1835 Hardwicke published two volumes of *Illustrations of Indian Zoology,* consisting of 202 colour plates from his art collection. Hardwicke, like most of those in the service of the Company who created collections of drawings, was not the artist. His works were collated from a whole army of artists whom he commissioned to draw for him, as well those interested persons who sent him drawings they acquired while on their travels or stationed in other parts of Asia.

An equally enthusiastic zoologist and devoted collector of specimens was Brian Hodgson, who at the tender age of 15 went to Haileybury College to train as a future civil servant for the Company. After two years at the college he travelled to Calcutta to complete his education at Fort William where he studied under the political economist Thomas Malthus. Because of ill health he was stationed in Nepal and spent most of his years there, rising to the post of Resident to Kathmandu before he retired from the service in 1844 and returned to England. Hodgson was an excellent linguist, being more than proficient in Bengali, Persian, Hindi, Nepali and Newari. He took a scholarly interest in Buddhist scriptures and all aspects of natural history, excelling particularly in ornithology. He wrote a great many zoological papers and is responsible for describing at least 150 bird species. Hodgson's interest in birds included collecting drawings as well as specimens. He wrote to his sister Fanny, that he had 'three native artists always employed in drawing from nature'.[2] He also kept a live tiger, four bears and three civets within his menagerie. The drawing collection he accumulated numbered in the thousands as did his collection of zoological specimens.

Hodgson travelled back to India in a private capacity in 1845 and settled in Darjeeling, on the frontier between British India and Sikkim. Here he devoted his time to studying the zoology of the Himalayas and ethnographic differences of the people of Northern India based on language. He was opposed to making English the primary language for education and administration in India, defending the use of the vernacular. During his years spent in Nepal, Hodgson became increasingly assimilated into the community. He adopted Nepali dress and abstained from meat and alcohol. These were also years in which European women were not allowed into Nepal. As the father of at least two children and possibly three, it is not surprising to learn that their mother was a local Nepalese woman called Meharrunisha Begum. In 1858 Hodgson left India for good and settled in England where he lived for a further very active 34 years.

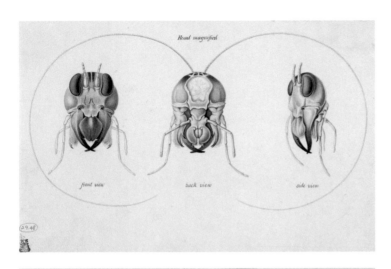

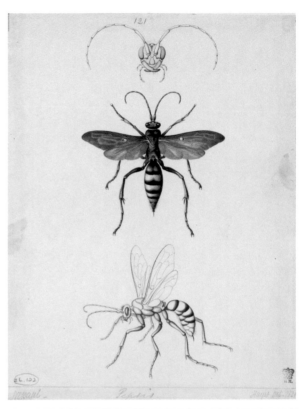

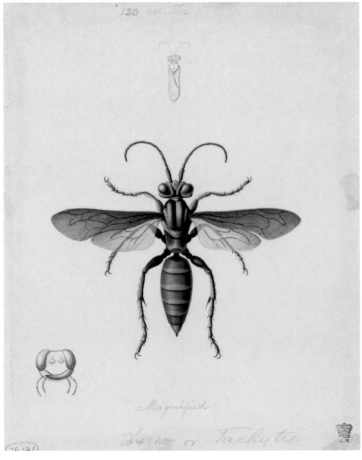

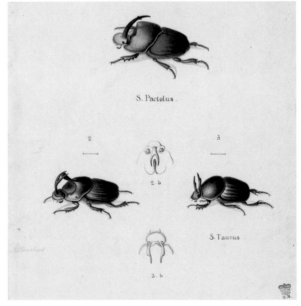

RIGHT Brian Hodgson
was at the forefront of
the study of Nepalese and
Tibetan fauna. He published
papers on a range of
zoological subjects and was
responsible for discovering
and describing a total of 22
new species of mammals
and 80 species of birds. He
also studied insects, reptiles
and fish.

BRIAN HOUGHTON
HODGSON COLLECTION
Indian rhinoceros,
Rhinoceros unicornis
Pencil and watercolour,
c.1850
284 x 470 mm

One of the more famous visitors Hodgson received when living in Darjeeling was Joseph
Dalton Hooker, close friend of Charles Darwin, correspondent of Alexander Humboldt and the son
of the botanist Sir William Hooker, Director of the Royal Botanic Gardens at Kew. From a young
age Hooker had attended his father's lectures and developed a keen interest in botany. He was also
captivated by the tales of the voyages of exploration of Captain Cook and Darwin's *Beagle* voyage
and, like others before him, dreamed of being part of an expedition to unknown regions of the globe.
Soon after graduating from Glasgow University with a medical degree he joined the Naval Medical
Service and accompanied James Clark Ross on an expedition to Antarctica on HMS *Erubus*, visiting
South America, South Africa, Australia and New Zealand. His work resulting from these travels won
him the acclaim of his peers and in 1847 he was elected a Fellow of the Royal Society. That same year
he received a stipend from government Treasury worth £400 per annum for two years, to collect plants
for Kew Gardens from the Himalayas, the first European to do so. Hooker ended up spending three
years in the Himalayas and received a further £300 as a salary for the additional 12 months. Accepting
the invitation from Hodgson to stay with him in Darjeeling, Hooker arrived at his hill-station residence

in 1848 and made it his base for two whole years. From Hodgson's house Hooker would embark on expeditions deep into Nepal and Sikkim and he even crossed into Tibet, a venture that angered the Rajah of Sikkim who promptly had him arrested. His release came only with the threatened intervention of the British military.

Hooker found the flora of the regions spectacular and was so struck by the rhododendrons that he produced a beautiful colour plate book on them. The publication of the book resulted in a great demand for the plants and they soon became a popular feature of Victorian gardens. The drawings that appeared in Hooker's *Himalayan Journals* were his own work, whilst the hand-coloured lithographs of rhododendrons were by the Scottish artist Walter Hood Fitch from sketches by Hooker. Hooker succeeded his father as Director of the Royal Botanic Gardens at Kew and was regarded as one of the most eminent botanists of his day.

Although Indian artists in the pay of the East India Company executed the majority of natural history art, there is a small but significant group of travellers, explorers or temporary residents in India that has contributed to the science and its illustration. These artists include a number of skilled draughtswomen who often possessed an excellent knowledge of the local natural history. Margaret Fountaine was born in Norwich, England, and travelled to India in 1912 after years spent exploring parts of Africa, the Middle East and Central America. Her main passion was the study of butterflies and she collected over 22,000 specimens during her lifetime whilst also producing a series of beautiful sketchbooks depicting the life cycle of different species. Another English woman artist who spent five years travelling through India was Olivia Tonge. At the age of 50 she set off on an adventure intent on studying and drawing all the exotic animals she encountered. During her time there she kept pets including a young crocodile that she named Cupid and 'a little jungle Hedge Hog'. These women naturalist artists are often dismissed as eccentrics but their understanding of the natural world was equal to many of the men who became well known within scientific circles and were considered serious scholars.

SNOW BEDS AT 13,000 FT. IN THE TH'LONOK VALLEY, WITH RHODODENDRONS KINCHINJUNGA IN THE DISTANCE.

ABOVE This is one of several sketches by Hooker made during his expedition to northern India.

JOSEPH DALTON HOOKER
Snow beds at 13,000 ft
Himalayan Journals, 1854
Lithograph
183 x 117 mm

OPPOSITE AND ABOVE *Hortus Malabacarus* is a wonderful
display of early botanical illustration from the seventeenth
century, predating Linnaeus and his classification system
based on the sexual characteristics of plants. The copper plate
engravings were hand coloured and make up a total 794 pages
of illustrations. It remained the most authoritative work on
Indian flora until the late eighteenth century.

HORTUS MALABARACUS
Solanum
Watercolour, 1750
413 x 280 mm

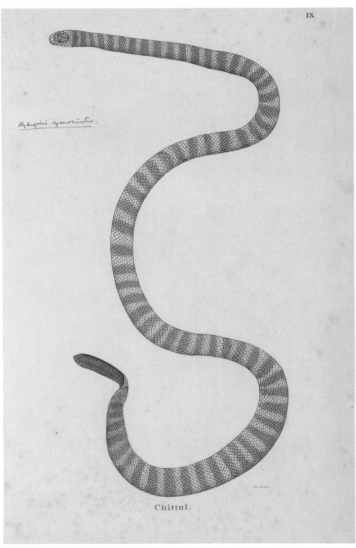

PATRICK RUSSELL
Short-nosed vine snake,
Ahaetulla prasina
An account of Indian
Serpents collected on the
coast of Coromandel, 1796
Hand-coloured engraving
515 x 360 mm

PATRICK RUSSELL
Annulated sea snake,
Hydrophis cyanocinctus
An account of Indian
Serpents collected on the
coast of Coromandel, 1796
Hand-coloured engraving
515 x 360 mm

OPPOSITE AND LEFT

Patrick Russell took an interest in all aspects of natural history. He collected botanical and zoological illustrations and also prepared snake skins mounted on paper, as in the example depicted on the near left. He wrote the preface to Roxburgh's *Plants of the Coast of Coromandel* in 1795 and published his own work on fish and reptiles of the same region. The drawings for his work on snakes were by several artists and include Alexander Russell who undertook all the illustrations for the second volume.

PATRICK RUSSELL
COLLECTION
Banded krait, *Bungarus fasciatus*
Skin and varnish, c.1790
525 x 390 mm

SWIETENIA FEBRIFUGA

LEFT AND ABOVE William Roxburgh is considered one of the most important figures in Indian botany. His work on describing plants, together with the supervision of their illustration by Indian artists in the early years of the nineteenth century, was the basis for all taxonomic research in Indian and southeast Asian botany for the following 50 years. Over 2,500 watercolour paintings were produced under his direction, including the *Allophylus* displayed above and possibly the *Soymida*, left, that forms part of a miscellaneous collection of Indian drawings.

INDIAN COLLECTION
Rohan bark, *Soymida febrifuga*
Watercolour, c.1800s
410 x 498 mm

WILLIAM ROXBURGH COLLECTION
Allophylus racemosus
Watercolour, c.1805
460 x 308 mm

RIGHT John Fleming was a surgeon in the East India Company. After the death of Colonel Kyd, the superintendant of the Calcutta Garden, in May 1793, Fleming was appointed as temporary superintendent until William Roxburgh took up the permanent post in November. Roxburgh arranged for many of his watercolour drawings to be copied and presented to his friends, one of whom was John Fleming. Fleming ended up with a collection of over a thousand illustrations of plants including this drawing of *Hibiscus cannabinus*.

JOHN FLEMING
COLLECTION
Ambary, *Hibiscus cannabinus*
Watercolour, *c.*1795–1805
457 x 312 mm

INDIAN DRAWINGS
FORMERLY THE PROPERTY OF
DR. JOHN FLEMING
Purchased 1882

Nymphaea rubra M.
Sundhi-Hala H.
Racta Sandhuca. Sans.

LEFT This stunning portrait of the nocturnal flowering plant Red Indian water lily, is yet another drawing from the Fleming collection. This species of lotus is of economic value as its roots and seeds can be eaten. This drawing was included in Roxburgh's *Plants of the Coast of Coromandel*.

JOHN FLEMING
COLLECTION
Red Indian water lily,
Nymphaea rubra
Watercolour, c.1795–1805
470 x 301 mm

RIGHT The ivy or scarlet-fruited gourd is widely distributed throughout the tropics. It is an economic plant that is cultivated in India and used mainly as a food plant, particularly the sweet fruits, although it also has some medicinal properties.

JOHN FLEMING COLLECTION
The ivy or scarlet-fruited gourd, *Coccinia grandis*
Watercolour, c.1795–1805
457 x 295 mm

The Saharunpore Botanical Garden in northern India was one of four gardens of the East India Company. Several of the superintendents of the garden employed artists to illustrate the plants brought to the garden from the collecting expeditions, particularly in the Himalayas. *Passiflora kermesina* is an example of one of these drawings, but unlike most of the plants, which were native to India, this plant originated from Brazil and was introduced to the garden from Europe.

SAHARUNPORE GARDEN
COLLECTION
Passiflora, *Passiflora kermesina*
Watercolour, c.1850
463 x 304 mm

LEFT The great many arthropod drawings in Thomas Hardwicke's collection are noted particularly for their exquisite beauty and precise accuracy and detail. Many of the drawings, including this tarantula , were produced by the artist known only as J. Hayes.

THOMAS HARDWICKE
COLLECTION [J. Hayes]
Spider
Watercolour, c.1820
272 x 203 mm

CHAMÆLEON

ABOVE The majority of the zoological drawings were taken from dead specimens but some of the animals are known to have been living, and the chameleon depicted here is one such example that was found in the Calcutta garden. 'The animal is exhibited under this colour as one of the various shades under which it showed itself – when in the garden.'

OPPOSITE Hardwicke's collection of drawings was equal to that of his specimens, and covered all branches of both vertebrate and invertebrate zoology. More than 800 drawings of insects from all regions of Asia helped form one of the most noted zoological collections of the nineteenth century from the Indian sub-continent.

THOMAS HARDWICKE
COLLECTION
Indian chameleon,
Chamaeleo zeylanicus
Watercolour, 1819
237 x 414 mm

THOMAS HARDWICKE
COLLECTION
Mantis
Watercolour, *c.*1820
331 x 267 mm

80

26.81

RIGHT This splendid illustration of a porcupine is drawn at a third of its natural size. It was one of the drawings selected and copied by Benjamin Waterhouse Hawkins for John Edward Gray's *Illustrations of Indian Zoology*, published in 1830–1834. The lithograph by Hawkins fails to capture the richness and depth of the original watercolour.

THOMAS HARDWICKE
COLLECTION
Crested porcupine,
Hystrix cristata
Watercolour, 1823
270 x 425 mm

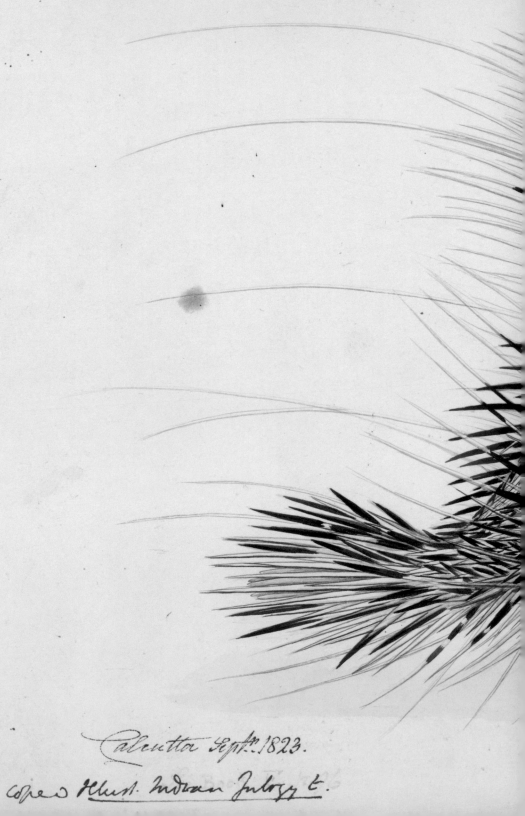

Hystrix Cristata
Common Porcupine
1/3.d the Nat: Size

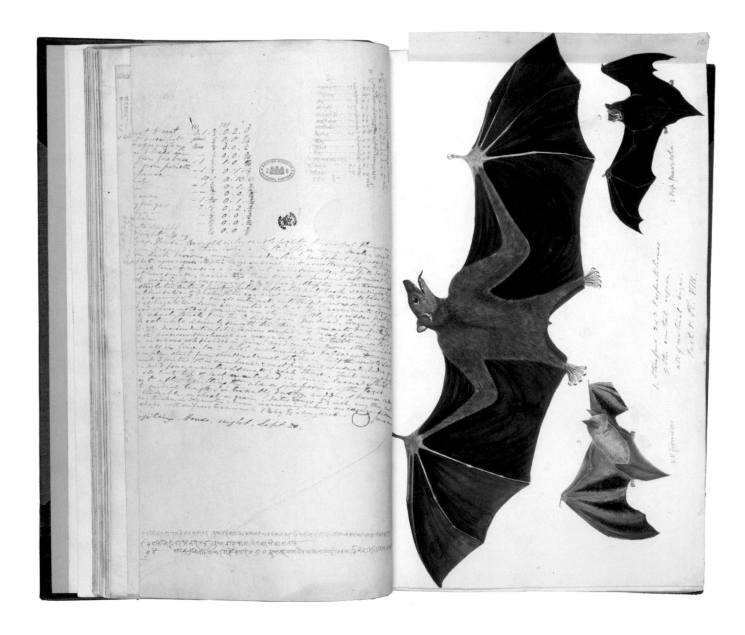

OPPOSITE The descriptive notes for many of Hodgson's bat drawings include not only measurements but also weight. Hodgson was held in high regard by many naturalists, including Charles Darwin and Sir Joseph Hooker, who named a species of rhododendron after him.

BRIAN HOUGHTON HODGSON COLLECTION
Flying fox, *Pteropus* sp. Hodgson's myotis, *Myotis formosus*
Nepalese whiskered myotis, *Myotis muricola*
Watercolour, *c.*1850s
285 x 490 mm

ABOVE Hodgson possessed one of the largest collections of Indian bird specimens, from all over the Himalayas and Nepal. Some were collected by him but he also relied extensively on Nepali trappers. As well as a scientific description, Hodgson provided details on the behaviour and habitat of a species.

BRIAN HOUGHTON HODGSON COLLECTION
Nutcracker, *Nucifraga caryocatactes*
Watercolour and pencil, *c.*1850s
290 x 470 mm

Capra Quadri mammis nob. mas.
The Jharal or Serow or Hemalay.
Extra Sheet XLVII

LEFT The Himalayan tahr is found throughout the Himalayas from northern India to Tibet and is specially adapted to life on the rugged mountains. This drawing depicts a family of tahs, the male with its typical distinguished ruff and the single offspring, which may remain with the mother for up to two years.

BRIAN HOUGHTON
HODGSON COLLECTION
Himalayan tahr,
Hemitragus jemlahicus
Watercolour, *c*.1850s
284 x 470 mm

ABOVE Few of the Indian artists employed to draw for Europeans are identified by name. Of those that are, the best known is Rajman Singh who worked for several Europeans including Brian Hodgson. Rajman completed many watercolour drawings of Himalayan and Nepalese birds and mammals of which two examples are depicted here.

RAJMAN SINGH
Satyr tragopan,
Tragopan satyra
Watercolour and bodycolour,
c.1850s
255 x 358 mm

RAJMAN SINGH
White-eared pheasant,
Crossoptilon crossoptilon
Watercolour and bodycolour,
c.1850s
290 x 352 mm

RIGHT AND OPPOSITE

Olivia Tonge was an accomplished watercolour painter from an early age, specializing in flowers, birds and reptiles. After the death of her husband Tonge travelled to India, accompanied by her daughter. There she produced 16 beautiful sketchbooks bursting with colourful drawings of plants and animals alongside personal artefacts such as Indian jewellery, household items and musical instruments.

Clockwise from top left:

OLIVIA TONGE
Palm squirrel,
Funambulus sp.
Watercolour, c.1912
180 x 258 mm

OLIVIA TONGE
Muggers, *Crocodylus palnotris*
Watercolour, c.1912
180 x 258 mm

OLIVIA TONGE
Pomelo
Watercolour, c.1912
180 x 258 mm

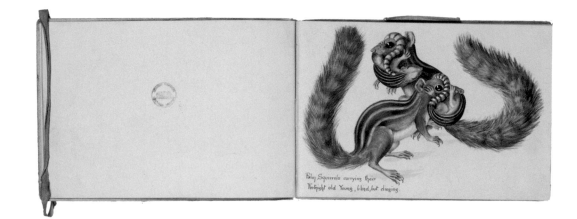

A Beetle
from
Mussoorie.

A fine ripe Pomelo,
peeled and cut
ornamentally for
Table by a clever
Khansamah.
They
are very
fond of
making
the dining
table

pretty.

ASIA:
Trade and Empire ~ **China**

THE BRITISH EAST INDIA COMPANY had been trading in China from the beginning of the eighteenth century. Whilst Europeans were for the most part accepted in India, and Indian and European relations gradually improved during this period, in China European traders remained segregated and were treated with suspicion. From 1757 the Qing Emperors confined trade between Europeans and Chinese to the Port of Canton during the trading season that ran from October to March. In the summer, Europeans were forced to leave the port and would usually spend those months in Macao. Trade could only be conducted through the official body of Chinese merchants called the Hong; these were family-owned trading houses licensed by the Chinese government. All European traders had to submit their requests to this body.

European knowledge of China had been filtering out for several centuries with the importation of silk, tea and spices. In the mid- to late seventeenth century artefacts such as Chinese furniture, fabric and porcelain also started to arrive in Europe in much greater quantity. By the mid-eighteenth century craftsmen in Europe began to copy the decorative Chinese style and motifs, and Chinese plants started to appear in English gardens. But Europeans were less familiar with the natural history of China and naturalists found it almost impossible to gain access to collect or survey any part of the Chinese mainland. Attempts by the British to establish trade and diplomatic relations with China were made with two missions, the first led by Lord Macartney in 1793; the second in 1816 under the authority of Earl Amherst. On each occasion Sir Joseph Banks was able to assign gardeners to the delegation with instructions to search out plants 'either useful, curious, or beautiful'. Neither the trade negotiations nor the plant collecting proved to be of much success.

The Company held a monopoly of British trade in Canton until 1833, exchanging spices, ivory and other products from India for Chinese tea and silk. Most of the products on offer by the Company were little sought after by the Chinese and Britain was more often than not forced to purchase their goods with silver. Conditions for European traders in Canton were uncomfortable and difficult. They were allowed access within the port only around the factory area, a series of warehouses reserved for foreign traders built alongside the river. All Europeans were prohibited from entering the walled city. Canton port was a bustling, thriving place during the trading season with traders from around the world including many merchants from other parts of China. Anything and everything was sold in the market place, plants and animals amongst them. Live animals and birds, skins, shells, minerals, plants and seeds were all traded on the international market. The plants came from all over China and were not always destined for European gardens as the Chinese had a long and popular tradition of gardening and horticulture.

Amongst the young men employed by the Company in Canton were some who took an active interest in natural history. These amateur naturalists relied on commercial contact with local Chinese for specimens and natural history knowledge. Such exchanges were extensive, albeit often controlled, and included not only merchants and officials, but also their servants, gardeners, craftsmen and interpreters. Contact with other Chinese in Canton such as fishermen, farmers, peasants and even monks all took place at some time or other, and each contributed to the transfer of knowledge from Chinese to Europeans. The plant nurseries in Canton, called Fa-tee, were famous in European horticultural circles by the early nineteenth century. Many Chinese plants introduced into Europe at this time came from these nurseries and as a consequence were cultivars rather than native wild plants of the region. As the century progressed there was growing demand for Chinese plants and animals from European scientists, naturalists and the public, together with an increased desire for knowledge of Chinese horticulture. The Hong merchants usually owned splendid gardens with rare plants that were not available in the nurseries. In these gardens they would regularly entertain foreign merchants and western visitors who found the gardens charming and who could, on occasion, benefit from a gift of a particularly coveted plant.

Of all those in the service of the Company who actively worked to further European knowledge of Chinese natural history, the English-born John Reeves is probably the best known. Reeves arrived in Canton in 1812 as Assistant Tea Inspector for the Canton factory. Reeves received no education in science and his understanding of taxonomy and animal anatomy never extended beyond the bare minimum. Nevertheless, he was a member of the Zoological and Horticultural Society in London and in 1817 was elected a Fellow of the Royal Society and Linnean Society, with scientists consulting with him about Chinese animals and plants throughout his life. When he first arrived in Canton, Reeves wasted little time in developing relations with those interested in the natural sciences, both Chinese and westerners. He visited the Fa-tee nurseries, market places, Hong merchants and the whole array of professionals who had something to sell or exchange. He also developed friendships with westerners resident in Macao, some

REEVES ZOOLOGICAL COLLECTION
Unidentified frog
Watercolour, c.1820s
354 x 444 mm

THE FACTORIES,

CANTON.

1856.

of whom had exotic gardens, menageries and aviaries. From all of these contacts Reeves was able to build up a regular supply of specimens that he shipped to Britain. Throughout his residence in Canton or Macau, some 19 years in all, Reeves shipped thousands of plants to Britain though, unfortunately, most of them died en route.

The most significant and long-lasting effect Reeves had on the natural sciences was through his commissioning and collecting of natural history illustrations. By the time Reeves arrived in Canton a thriving industry producing artefacts for the western market had already become established. Numerous workshops existed employing generations of family members of artists and artisans. Embarking on his project of collecting natural history illustrations, Reeves had no problem in finding artists for the work. Skilled and talented artists were abundant but scientific accuracy was not usually a feature of Chinese art so Reeves provided instruction in the subject, detailing the conventions for botanical and zoological illustration. These drawings differed from the traditional artwork created for the European market which were ornamental, highly stylized depictions of flora and fauna usually set in a scenic background. Reeves's drawings rarely have any background and tend to be single specimens on a plain sheet. The botanical drawings often include magnified, floral details of the plant but for most of the animal drawings there is little if any anatomical detail.

Reeves sent his drawings to various patrons, horticultural societies and botanical gardens in Britain. One of his main correspondents and supporters was Sir Joseph Banks who was particularly keen that drawings were made of the plants, as he knew that few of the living specimens would survive the journey. The drawings portray plants, fruits and cultivated flowers that were so popular amongst the British. Also included were depictions of insects, reptiles, amphibians, birds and mammals, some of which were not native to China, or even Asia, but had found their way into the collections through the street markets of Canton and Macao. John Reeves was not the only westerner to employ Chinese artists to illustrate the local flora and fauna, but he was certainly the most productive and best known amongst his British associates. In 1827 Reeves was joined by his son, John Russell, who succeeded his father as enthusiastic gatherer of all things pertaining to natural history. After Reeves left China for good in 1831, his son took over his mantle as naturalist for the scientists and institutions in his home country.

OPPOSITE This drawing of Canton is from a volume of botanical drawings by a local artist, which was commissioned by Henry Fletcher Hance in the 1850s. Hance was a British diplomat posted first to Hong Kong in 1844 and then to Whampoa in 1861 and later to Canton in 1878. He had a broad interest in natural history, particularly botany, and corresponded with Charles Darwin, sending him specimens. The drawing figures a typical factory in Canton, similar to those of the East India Company when John Reeves was working as a tea inspector earlier in the nineteenth century.

HENRY FLETCHER HANCE
Canton
Watercolour and bodycolour,
c.1853
125 x 175 mm

LEFT AND BELOW Chinese export painting was, by the early nineteenth century, a large and important industry which had expanded alongside the growing China trade. The traditional paintings made for export bore a distinct stylistic hallmark with the use of bright colours and strong outline, which produce a flat appearance and were considered not very accurate. The studios and factories producing these paintings and highly decorative artefacts were usually family run and included several generations, whereby the younger members were apprenticed to their older masters for several years to learn the skills. It was these artists that John Reeves approached to prepare his illustrations of plants and animals.

JOHN REEVES COLLECTION
Lion-haired macaque, *Macaca silenus*
Watercolour, c.1820s
466 x 590 mm

JOHN REEVES COLLECTION
Bengal slow loris, *Nycticebus bengalensis*
Watercolour, c.1820s
542 x 465 mm

蟹山

紅沙馬

花娘蟹

馬仔蟹

白蟹

炉蟹

蟹肉

蟹石

蟹羅琴

老虎蟹

LEFT For almost 20 years John Reeves dedicated much of his time to investigating the natural history of China and commissioning and compiling one of the largest collections of natural history artwork. Hundreds of drawings of plants, insects, birds, mammals, molluscs, fish and crustaceans were collated through the energies of this one man.

JOHN REEVES COLLECTION
Crustaceans
Watercolour, c.1820s
385 x 494 mm

RIGHT AND OPPOSITE

Both of these drawings are unsigned and indeed most of the Chinese artists who produced natural history drawings for Europeans are little known. The red lionfish (opposite) is a venomous coral reef fish, with the venom contained in the long, separated dorsal spines. Reeves's illustrations were an important source for taxonomic researches. Sir John Richardson identified over 70 new species of fish from the drawings.

JOHN REEVES COLLECTION
Molluscs
Watercolour, c.1820s
378 x 486 mm

JOHN REEVES COLLECTION
The red lionfish,
Pterois volitans
Watercolour, c.1820s
380 x 485 mm

魚岳　魚鬸

OPPOSITE The Eurasian eagle owl is a large bird with vivid orange eyes and pointed prominent ear tufts.

ABOVE The red-crowned crane is significant in Chinese culture as it is the symbol of longevity. The delicate delineation of this drawing captures the elegant splendour of this bird. This crane is, unfortunately, now one of the most endangered species of bird.

JOHN REEVES COLLECTION
Eagle owl, *Bubo bubo*
Watercolour, c.1820s
585 x 478 mm

JOHN REEVES COLLECTION
Red-crowned crane,
Grus japonensis
Watercolour, c.1820s
380 x 485 mm

Urania speciosa   170.

OPPOSITE AND RIGHT The Reeves botanical drawings differed from the export paintings produced for the western market, in that they were usually more accurate and the subject was depicted in isolation with no background. John Reeves gave instructions to his artists on what parts of the plants he required them to draw, to aid the scientists in Europe. This was not something Chinese artists were familiar with as the closest they came to making botanical drawings was preparing horticultural illustrations. With them the emphasis was on the form and colour of a particular specimen or variety of flower, the purpose of which was to exhibit the latest collection of plants growing in the local nurseries.

JOHN REEVES COLLECTION
Palm, *Urania specosa*
Watercolour, *c.*1820s
490 x 384 mm

JOHN REEVES COLLECTION
Sacred lotus, *Nelumbo nucifera*
Watercolour, *c.*1820s
460 x 374 mm

Africa

FORSTER **MASSON** RAPER **HARRIS** BERNATZ **BAINES** FINCH-DAVIES **TALBOT**

UNTAINE FORSTER **MASSON** RAPER **HARRIS** BERNATZ **BAINES** FINCH-DAVIES

AFRICA:
From Enlightenment to Victorian Exploration

EUROPEAN PRESENCE IN AFRICA DATES BACK to the fifteenth century, with the beginnings of the European slave trade. But it was only by the seventeenth century that the Dutch, Portuguese, French and English had really established their trading stations along the coastlines of the continent. The trading companies dealt in people as well as minerals, ivory and other products and, in some regions, introduced plants and crops, particularly from the New World. British involvement in Africa up to the end of the eighteenth century was limited to a series of chartered trading companies such as the Royal African Company and the African Company of Merchants. Fortresses were built along the western coast of Africa as stations for Company officers and trading ships. These companies maintained control through economic dominance in the region and it was not until the mid- to late nineteenth century that direct crown rule by the British developed as a result of competition with other European countries.

Despite their familiarity with the coastal regions of Africa, Europeans' knowledge of what lay inland was next to nothing in the eighteenth century. On June 9th 1788 a group of some of the most prominent men in Britain met to form 'themselves into an Association for promoting the discovery of the inland parts of that quarter of the world'.[1] It became known as the African Association and Sir Joseph Banks was its treasurer. Its main purpose was that of exploration, to gain knowledge of the geography of the African interior rather than for trade, and the Association sponsored several explorations including the first expedition of Mungo Park, who set out to discover the course of the Niger river. The African Association heralded the age of exploration of the continent that blossomed in the mid-nineteenth century. By then expeditions to parts of Africa gripped the imagination of the Victorian public with a previously unseen fervour, whilst also making national heroes of some of the explorers.

One of the key strategic locations for Europeans in Africa was Cape Town, on the southern tip of the continent. The Dutch East India Company occupied the area as early as the mid-eighteenth century. In 1795 the British captured Cape Town from the Dutch but then lost it again in 1803 before re-taking it in 1806. During the eighteenth and nineteenth centuries, when the Dutch and British dominated the trade between Asia and Europe, the Cape was an important location for sea-going vessels to find respite and make repairs. It also served as a safe haven for vessels going further afield to the unchartered areas of the Southern Ocean. This was so for Cook's second voyage in 1772–1775 when he was the commander of HMS *Resolution*. On board were German naturalist Johann Forster and his son Georg who were appointed 'in order to collect, describe, and draw the objects of natural history'.[2] Much of the voyage was spent on the open seas criss-crossing the Antarctic Ocean where Georg Forster sketched and painted terns, petrels, penguins, albatrosses and other sea birds. Visits to land were few and far between and Forster had to make the best use of his time in recording the wildlife he encountered. After leaving Portsmouth in July 1772 the *Resolution* arrived in Cape Town in October. It spent three weeks on this first visit to Cape Town and a further five weeks in 1775 on the return journey. Inland exploration was restricted and the Forsters bemoaned the fact that they had little time to collect specimens. Rather than studying animals in the wild, Georg had to rely on observing animals held in captivity in the Company garden. Travelling on the outward journey was the botanist Francis Masson who had been commissioned by the Royal Botanic Gardens at Kew to collect plants and seed. He left the ship on its first arrival at the Cape and spent the next three years conducting botanical surveys in southern Africa and collecting some exotic and beautiful plants to grow at Kew. Masson returned to Cape Town to continue his work in 1786 and remained there until 1795.

By 1833 the East India Company had lost its monopoly as a trading institution and had ceased to be a trading body in India altogether. It was now entrusted with running the colonial administration in India and continued to organize surveys and expeditions including trade missions for the British outside of India or Southeast Asia. In 1841 the Company received an invitation from King Sahla Sellasie of the kingdom of Shewa in Ethiopia and organized a diplomatic mission to the region. The Company selected Captain William Cornwallis Harris to lead this expedition. Harris had by this date made a name for himself through publishing *The Wild Sports of Southern Africa* in 1839, which told of his hunting expeditions from 1836 to 1837. He was a member of the Engineering Corps of the East India Company and was based in India from 1825. In 1836 he fell ill and was sent to Cape Town to recuperate. His expedition to the interior of southern Africa was primarily for hunting purposes and, as Harris explained in the opening passage of his book, 'From my boyhood upwards I have been taxed by the

CLAUDE FINCH-DAVIES
Hartebeest, *Alcelaphus buselaphus*
Watercolour, c.1913
195 x 144 mm

facetious with *shooting madness*, and truly a most delightful mania I have ever found it'.[3] Also from a young age Harris frequently found his 'thoughts wander to the wilds of Africa' and he often dreamed of meeting with the animals of that land, particularly the 'slender and swan-like neck of the stately giraffe' and the 'gigantic elephants'.[4] His account of the trip is full of hunting exploits and this has earned him the reputation as the originator of Safari. His work also records a great deal of information about the early stages of the Great Trek by the Voortrekkers, and his encounters with Mzilikazi, chief of the Matabele nation, when based at Mosega in the Marico Valley. Harris was a keen naturalist and an accomplished artist and includes in his book descriptions of the animals of the region together with illustrations.

The British expedition led by Harris to the court of King Sahla Sellasie, was a diplomatic 'Embassy'. Its purpose was to conclude an international treaty that would give Britain unrestricted commercial access to the region and its trade routes. The East India Company had taken control of the Port of Aden in 1839, and a treaty with the Christian Kingdom of Shewa was seen as a way of protecting British trade routes. Amongst the Embassy members were Johann Martin Bernatz, the official artist, and Rupert Kirk, the assistant surgeon who also produced maps and drawings from the expedition. Bernatz was born in Speyer in southern Germany and spent the years 1836 to 1837 travelling in the Levant. On his return to Germany he published his drawings in a work called *Scenes in the Holy Land* and then decided to produce a similar work, but on a grander scale, from his travels in India. This project proved more difficult than he first envisaged, so that when he was offered the post of artist on Harris's expedition he was more than happy to accept it.

The journey to the highlands was difficult, dangerous and not without major disruptions. In June the party travelled by camel from Tadjoura on the coast to Ankober, the capital of the kingdom of Shewa, a journey of 370 miles. Harris was unable to secure enough camels for the journey so part of the Embassy had to stay behind in Tadjoura. This remaining group included Bernatz who arrived in Ankober in March of the following year. As the first party set off across the lowlands tragedy struck when three members of the group were murdered. Despite these setbacks Harris succeeded in delivering to the British a signed treaty between Sahla Sellasie and the Queen of England, dated 16th November 1841. The Embassy remained in the region for another year and some of its members were able to observe several important festivals in the Shewa and Christian calendar; these were recorded in the drawings of Harris, Bernatz and Kirk. In February 1843 the Embassy left Shewa for India and the following year Harris published his book *Highlands of Ethiopia* and was knighted by the Queen for his accomplishments. Harris's life was sadly cut short in 1848 when he died of a 'lingering fever' in India, aged 41. Bernatz, who had been left in Aden on the return journey to recover from

illness, made several further expeditions including a visit to Egypt and Palestine. He eventually settled in his native Germany where he continued to paint and pursue his studies of the Orient. Many of his drawings from the Shewa expedition depict the ethnic diversity of the people and are some of the earliest observations by Europeans of life in Ethiopia. In 1852 Bernatz published some of his drawings in *Scenes of Ethiopia* which also included extracts of his journal from the expedition.

While Harris and Bernatz were busy observing and drawing in Ethiopia in 1842, a young Thomas Baines from Norfolk, England, was sailing on the schooner *Olivia* to Cape Town where he hoped to make a living as an ornamental artist. Baines was a good enough painter to progress to being a marine and portrait artist and, from 1845 to 1848, he managed to receive enough commissions to keep him at the Cape. In 1848 Baines experienced his first taste of travelling in southern Africa when he made the journey northeast from Cape Town across the Orange river and then on to the great Fish river. In 1850 he joined an expedition to explore Lake Ngami in present day Botswana. He then took up a post as the first official war artist to the British armed forces in South Africa and spent eight months travelling along the frontier. In all of these travels he completed oil paintings and watercolours. In 1855 he joined an expedition led by Augustus Gregory to Northern Australia. So impressed was Gregory with Baines that he named Mount Baines and Baines river after him. His standing as an excellent explorer and artist provided the opportunity for him to join the Royal Geographical Society sponsored expedition to the Zambezi river led by David Livingstone.

Baines was appointed artist-storekeeper to the expedition, which also included Livingstone's brother Charles, Dr John Kirk as surgeon and botanist and Richard Thornton as geologist. The expedition left Cape Town in April 1858 in high spirits. Soon, however, a disaster was to befall Baines that would ruin his future as an artist for any government supported exploration. In 1859 Baines contracted a fever and was confined to camp while Livingstone and Kirk went off exploring. Charles Livingstone was responsible for the camp while his brother was absent and accused Baines of theft of expedition property; a charge that is today viewed as wholly without foundation. In July 1859 Baines was dismissed from the expedition but had to submit himself to the degrading experience of remaining with the party for a further five months before he could obtain safe passage to Cape Town. During this time he was kept isolated, living in one of the whaleboats, and, as Livingstone would not allow Baines 'to come to our table', had his meals alone.

Baines spent years attempting to clear his name but never managed to get an official apology and never again secured Royal Geographical Society funding for his work. Despite this he continued to send drawings and information from his travels in South Africa to several institutions in Britain, including the Royal Botanic Gardens and the Royal Geographical Society. The latter organization

OPPOSITE This drawing is an example of collaborative work between Johann Martin Bernatz and the assistant surgeon, Rupert Kirk on the British expedition to the court of King Sahla Sellasie. Bernatz was enthralled by the 'Magnificent scenery in South Abyssinia Highlands'.

JOHANN MARTIN BERNATZ and RUPERT KIRK Watercolour and bodycolour, c.1841 230 x 290 mm

OPPOSITE This drawing

of the red-billed hornbill,

was completed in 1918.

Finch-Davies notes that

he found the species to

be common in southwest

Africa.

CLAUDE FINCH-DAVIES
Red-billed hornbill,
Tockus erythrorhynchus
Watercolour, 1918
195 x 144 mm

showed their appreciation of him in 1873 by presenting him with a gold watch for his continued service to geography. Baines continued to travel and explore South Africa, usually working for trading or mining companies, and he always took the opportunity to draw the wildlife he encountered. He was never an expert naturalist and rarely used scientific names for the species he drew. But he did read basic botanical books and acquired a fair understanding of the subject. He also took measurements of the animals he drew, wrote descriptions and noted observations of behaviour and habitat.

Baines died in 1875, one year after the birth of Claude Gibney Davies, one of the finest bird artists. Davies was born in Delhi, India and then sent to England for his education. From a very young age he took a keen interest in natural history and began drawing birds. At the age of 18 he enrolled as a private soldier with the Cape Mounted Riflemen and arrived in Cape Town in 1893. Southern Africa provided him with the opportunity to explore his interest in natural history and he spent much of his free time hunting, collecting and drawing birds. By the time Davies arrived in South Africa there were few birds that were not known to science and most had been identified, described and named. However little else about them had been recorded. Only a modest amount was known of species distribution and habits and, as a devoted ornithologist, Davies was intent on making his contribution to the overall knowledge of the subject. He cultivated contacts in museums that enabled him to study the collections of rare birds and he corresponded with ornithologists in South Africa and Britain.

In 1916 Davies married Aileen Singleton Finch, an only child and 20 years his junior. Her father insisted on Davies adopting the name of Finch and he willingly concurred, and from then on was known as Finch-Davies. Life was looking very promising for Finch-Davies who by then had been promoted to lieutenant. He was known for his artistic skills in wider circles as he had illustrated Major Boyd Robert Horsbrugh's book *Gamebirds and Waterfowl of South Africa*. By 1917 Finch-Davies was publishing papers in several key ornithological and natural history journals, often correcting previously poorly described species. He had also by then become an expert on the birds of prey of southern Africa, the study of which he was able to finance himself. By 1920 he and his wife had three children when disaster struck.

Finch-Davies carried out much of his work in the Transvaal Museum, studying their bird collections and working in the library. His work on South African raptors directed him to consult published colour plates of species for which he had no specimens. In December 1919 the librarian reported that plates were missing from a number of journals and the police were consulted. On the 5th January 1920 police observed Finch-Davies removing plates from reference books. No formal charges were pursued, but as a result of the discovery Finch-Davies handed over 29 of his sketchbooks with over 100 watercolour drawings to the museum as compensation. His regiment was also informed

C. G. Finch-Davies.
9-4-1918.

RIGHT From 1911–1912 Dorothy Talbot and her husband collected some 2,000 specimens of plants from the Oban district of southern Nigeria. One hundred and fifty of these were new to science and Dorothy produced life-size drawings of the rare and newly discovered plants. Talbot intended to publish colour plates of her drawings with descriptions of new genera and species, a project that was to be funded by the Royal Society, but the work never materialized.

DOROTHY TALBOT
Kola nut, *Cola sp.*
Watercolour, c.1911
700 x 368 mm

of the misdemeanour. Added to the shame and humiliation of the revelation, Finch-Davies' career was now in ruins. Within seven months Finch-Davies was dead. Although the cause of death was recorded as unknown, the note 'angina pectoris' was added in the margin of the death certificate. Finch-Davies's contribution to the knowledge of South African ornithology remains considerable, and he managed to display many facets of plumage, colour and texture in his exquisite drawings. Other bird artists admired his work and some of them transposed his drawings as lithographs and had them published.

By the twentieth century exploration of East and West Africa by Europeans was reaching its zenith. Amongst the numerous explorers were several women. Dorothy Talbot spent many years travelling with her husband, Percy Amaury, who worked for the Nigerian Political Service. Husband and wife explored large areas of West Africa, studying and writing about the natural history and the people of the region. In 1915 Dorothy published her book about the Ibibios women of southern Nigeria. Between them the Talbots collected thousands of plants, some of which were new to science, and Dorothy produced large watercolour paintings of many of them. Travelling in Algeria, East and West Africa at much the same time was the lepidopterist, Margaret Fountaine. She spent almost 50 years travelling the globe to collect and study butterflies and kept journals of her travels and produced beautiful sketchbooks filled with drawings of insects. For 27 of those years her constant companion was Khalil Neimy, an Egyptian born to Greek parents, whom she first met in Damascus. She later wrote that 'the most interesting part of my life was spent with him'. Between them they collected thousands of specimens from over 60 different countries and conducted studies on the life-cycle of butterflies. Fountaine was recognized by entomologists the world over and attended the Second International Congress of Entomologists held in Oxford in 1912. Her last days were spent collecting butterflies in Trinidad, where she died age 78 and where she is buried.

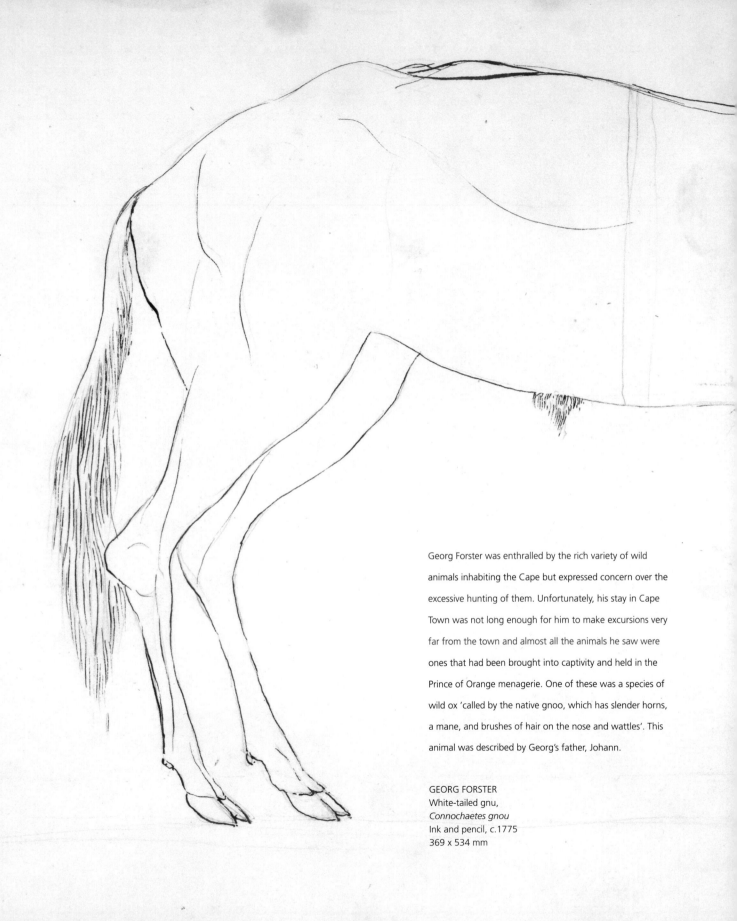

Georg Forster was enthralled by the rich variety of wild animals inhabiting the Cape but expressed concern over the excessive hunting of them. Unfortunately, his stay in Cape Town was not long enough for him to make excursions very far from the town and almost all the animals he saw were ones that had been brought into captivity and held in the Prince of Orange menagerie. One of these was a species of wild ox 'called by the native gnoo, which has slender horns, a mane, and brushes of hair on the nose and wattles'. This animal was described by Georg's father, Johann.

GEORG FORSTER
White-tailed gnu,
Connochaetes gnou
Ink and pencil, c.1775
369 x 534 mm

OPPOSITE, LEFT AND BELOW Cook's second voyage on HMS *Resolution* lasted three years and much of that time was spent at sea, criss-crossing the southern oceans and being 'obliged to content ourselves with the produce of a few small islands, which we could imperfectly investigate in the short spaces of sometimes a few hours, or a few days, or to the utmost of a few weeks, in unfavourable seasons'. All four drawings were produced in Cape Town, either during their three week stay in 1772 or their five week stay in 1775.

GEORG FORSTER
Cape teal, *Anas capensis*
Watercolour, 345 x 467 mm
Grey-headed lovebird, *Agapornis canus*
Watercolour, 541 x 367 mm
Spring hare, *Pedetes capensis*
Watercolour and pencil, 540 x 367 mm
Cape mole-rat, *Georychus capensis*
Watercolour, 369 x 540 mm

RIIGHT AND OPPOSITE

The Cape botanical garden was particularly important because it served as a depositary for plants transported between Asia and Europe or the Americas. At the Cape garden they would be replanted and hopefully recover, thereby improving their chances of survival. Francis Masson was often described by visitors as 'the King's botanical gardener'. He first visited the Cape in 1771 on board HMS *Resolution*. He remained there for three years and made three expeditions inland, collecting plants for the East India Company and for the Royal Botanic Gardens, Kew.

FRANCIS MASSON
Sea spider iris
Ferraria crispa
Watercolour, 1775
411 x 272 mm

FRANCIS MASSON
Traveller's Palm,
Ravenala madagascariensis
Watercolour, 1789
348 x 490 mm

All of these figures of the Zebra are excellent, but they are on too large a scale, and must be reduced to the size of the figure in the large drawing, which figure is to be cancelled.

OPPOSITE Harris believed that the drawings of large quadrupeds like zebra in natural history books were more often than not inaccurate. He explained that he had learnt to draw as a young boy by copying Thomas Bewick's woodcuts of animals, and his leisure time was devoted to 'making accurate portraits' of animals.

WILLIAM CORNWALLIS HARRIS
Cape mountain zebra, *Equus zebra*
Proof engraving, *c*.1838
198 x 309 mm

ABOVE 'Hunting the Giraffe.' On first sighting of a group of giraffes Harris's 'blood coursed through my veins like quicksilver'. He asked who could ride by the side of a troop of giraffes 'and not feel his spirits stirred within him?'

WILLIAM CORNWALLIS HARRIS
Giraffe, *Giraffa camelopardalis*
Colour lithograph, *c*.1836
144 x 225 mm

ABOVE This drawing is of the annual procession of clergy carrying traditional Ethiopian crosses from the church of St Michael, Ankobar. The church was built in 1825 by Sahla Sellasie, 1813–1847. Martin Bernatz explained in his published work that the parasol carried by the priest is the symbol of the church and that it is made from 'solid silver'.

JOHANN MARTIN BERNATZ
Cathedral of St Michael
Watercolour and
bodycolour, [1842]
230 x 290 mm

ABOVE Martin Bernatz described how after Lent the King kept an open table that lasted for a whole week and food was provided to every free man. It was a ritual that was significant for both political and religious reasons. The banquet depicted in this drawing takes place in the hall of the palace.

JOHANN MARTIN BERNATZ
Interior of Banquet Hall of the Palace
Watercolour and bodycolour, 1842
230 x 290 mm

LEFT Some of Bernatz's drawings were based on sketches made by the expedition leader William Harris. But Bernatz's distinct romantic and somewhat idealized style is evident in all his landscape paintings and portraits of human activity.

JOHANN MARTIN BERNATZ
Collecting water from the well
Watercolour, c.1842
230 x 290 mm

OPPOSITE AND LEFT

Bernatz was the Embassy's official artist but was one of a group that had to remain in Tadjoura for almost an additional five months until a sufficient number of camels and drivers was available to take them to the Highlands. Bernatz made his journey to the Kingdom of Shewa arriving in Ankober in March 1842. He recorded many of the scenes en route together with portraits of people from the different ethnic groups he encountered. In 1852 he published a volume of tinted lithographs based on his drawings and accompanying text, which was taken from his own journal.

JOHANN MARTIN BERNATZ
Male figure
Watercolour, c.1842
172 x 126 mm

JOHANN MARTIN BERNATZ
Female figure sitting
Pencil, c.1842
159 x 122 mm

ABOVE AND RIGHT The drawings of the wildebeest and the warthog were made from dead specimens but are both depicted as living animals, the warthog standing and the wildebeest in flight. Baines manages to capture beautifully and accurately the movement of the wildebeest, indicating how good an observer he was in the field.

THOMAS BAINES
White-tailed gnu,
Connochaetes gnou
Watercolour, 1869
268 x 383 mm

THOMAS BAINES
Desert warthog,
Phacochoerus aethiopicus
Watercolour and pencil,
c.1870
273 x 382 mm

RIGHT The legend inscribed at the bottom of this drawing reads 'Mangrove swamp at low water / mouth of the Kongone River / Zambesi Delta Nov 22nd / 1859 T Baines / The light tree is Doacenna / the long drops are the seeds of the mangrove / which pierce the soft mud when they fall / Rhizophora mucronata'. This drawing of the mangrove swamp was made during the Livingstone expedition in search of the Zambezi.

THOMAS BAINES
'Mangrove swamp'
Watercolour, 1859
377 x 264 mm

LEFT AND BELOW LEFT

After the Livingstone expedition Thomas Baines travelled on several occasions with the photographer James Chapman. Both men kept journals and published books about their expeditions, revealing how they assisted each other in their own artistic speciality and explaining how photography and painting and sketching complemented each other as methods of recording wildlife and natural scenes.

THOMAS BAINES
Head of crocodile
Pencil, watercolour and chalk, 1870
192 x 274 mm

THOMAS BAINES
Spotted hyaena,
Crocuta crocuta
Watercolour and pencil, 1870
273 x 382 mm

The Installation of NoBengula - into the Supreme chieftainship of Matabili land about a month
the young King exercising his first act of sovereignty by sacrificing cattle to the manes of his fat
at Inhklathlangela Monday May 22 - 1870 -

the death of his father Umselegasi (or Moselekatse) the Molimo or great spirit and for other causes
T. Baines.

ABOVE Thomas Baines produced landscape artworks, natural history drawings and also completed a large number of portraits of southern African people. Depicted here is Ingosi, the son of Um Nombati of Matabeleland.

LEFT The people of Matabeleland gather here to witness the installation of their new supreme chief, Notsengulu, in February 1870. Baines explains that the young king exercises his first act of sovereignty 'by sacrificing cattle to the names of his father'.

THOMAS BAINES
Instillation of Notsengulu
Pencil, 1870
272 x 381 mm

THOMAS BAINES
Ingosi, son of Um Nombati
Watercolour, 1869
392 x 281 mm

RIGHT Two pages from the twenty-one page sketchbook of Claude Finch-Davies depicting the great white pelican and the yellow-billed stork. The pelican is widespread across Africa. It is a large, heavy bird that inhabits inland waters and swamps, often feeding in flocks of great number. The stork, Finch-Davies explained, was 'a rare species south of the Zambezi'.

CLAUDE FINCH-DAVIES
Great white pelican,
Pelecanus onocrotalus
Watercolour, 1918
255 x 180 mm

CLAUDE FINCH-DAVIES
Yellow-billed stork,
Mycteria ibis
Watercolour, 1918
255 x 180 mm

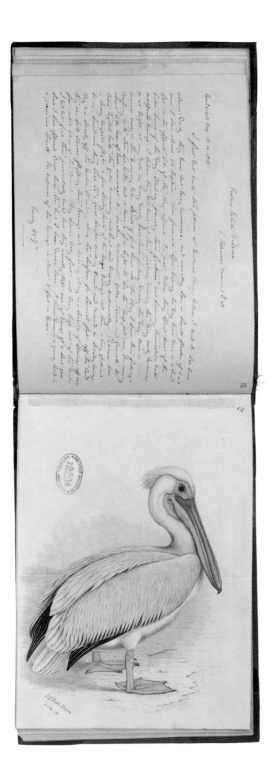

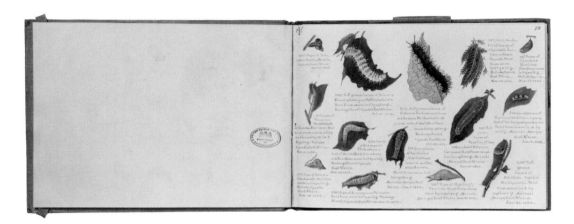

LEFT AND BELOW

Margaret Fountaine travelled the world, including Algeria and East and West Africa, in search of butterflies. Her sketchbooks produced from1907 to 1939 contain beautiful and detailed watercolour illustrations of butterfly larvae and pupae from around the globe. She placed each larva on the food plant the insect fed upon and indicated those species that were new to science.

MARGARET FOUNTAINE
Sketchbooks of Lepidoptera
Watercolour, 1907 -1939
Vol. 1: 127 x 180 mm
Vol. 4: 178 x 250 mm

Europe

DIETZSCH **EHRET** BAUER **AUBRIET** SPAENDONCK **REDOUTÉ** TYSON **PARSONS**

EUROPE:

European Visions of the Natural World

EXPANDING EMPIRES, IMPROVED NAUTICAL KNOWLEDGE and growing commercial trade between European nations and their colonies provided some artists with the opportunity to observe and draw plants and animals in their natural habitats. The colonial trade links also offered scientists and artists who remained in Europe the prospect of studying the flora and fauna of distant lands, albeit out of context. It was now possible for many naturalists to learn about hitherto unknown plants, animals and people without ever leaving their studies. From here they could impose upon the colonies the 'correct' scientific explanation of a country's natural history. The introduction of exotic plants and animals encouraged the re-creation of colonial landscapes in the gardens, aviaries and menageries of the wealthy as well as influencing the formation of public botanical and zoological gardens of the future. With the display of wonders of nature from around the world in one's parks and greenhouses, it was also possible to impress one's friends with hand-coloured volumes of botanical and zoological drawings.

The prospect for artists to earn a living from drawing nature was never better than in the eighteenth century, although many a talented draughtsman had to supplement his or her income by other means. Natural history art in all its forms was a growth industry. It was possible for some artists to find wealthy patrons or learned societies who would support their art through commissions or the purchase of existing drawings. Scientific drawings were increasingly in demand from an ever-broadening field of clients and, with the growth in publishing, more and more artists were able to find employment as painters, engravers or lithographers. Like the museum or laboratory naturalists who never ventured into the field, there were artists who illustrated accompanying text never having seen the species in its natural habitat or the landscape they placed it in. By the mid-nineteenth century this was increasingly common and included some of the most acclaimed illustrators such as John Gould and Walter Hood Fitch.

The boundary between still-life flower painting and botanical illustration can be difficult to distinguish, and this was particularly true in the first half of the eighteenth century. The Dutch and Flemish flower painters produced magnificent oil paintings of ornate bouquets of flowers placed in dramatic lighting. Many of these artists crossed over to produce wonderfully delicate watercolour drawings of single flowers, the purpose of which was to exhibit new cultivated varieties that were sold through various nurseries. Often generations of families were involved in such artistry and one of the more famous of them was the Dutch van Huysum family.

Similarly in Germany there were family dynasties of artists. Amongst the most well known and respected of the time was the Dietzsch family who came from Nuremburg, an important centre for botanical art in early eighteenth-century Europe. Several members of the family were Nuremburg court painters and a distinct feature of their work was the preparation of their paintings on a dark-brown or black background. The effect of the still-life flower painting tradition on the artist Maria Sibylla Merian is strikingly evident, whilst her work influenced later artists who straddled the two genres of art.

It was in Germany that some of the first scientific artists of the eighteenth century emerged, and amongst them was Georg Dionysius Ehret. Born in 1708 in Heidelberg, Ehret was apprenticed as a gardener for several years. He taught himself the technique of watercolour painting and with his knowledge of plants he decided at the age of 23 to seek his living as an artist and botanist. Ehret is considered the first artist to dedicate his work exclusively to the subject of botany and he became the finest and most celebrated botanical artist of his day. Before leaving Germany for good, Ehret spent time in Nuremburg where he met with the physician Christoph Jacob Trew, who became Ehret's patron and lifelong friend. In the 1730s Ehret travelled to Holland but eventually elected to settle in England, where he worked for many years in the gardens of wealthy patrons depicting newly introduced plants from around the world. When Joseph Banks returned to England from a visit to Newfoundland in 1766 he employed Ehret to illustrate the plants that he had collected.

The accolades bestowed on Ehret during and after his lifetime were not superseded until the work of the two Bauer brothers became known. Franz Bauer visited London in 1788 from his native Austria, with the intention of continuing his travels to Paris. His plans were disrupted by the intervention of Sir Joseph Banks who was so impressed with Bauer's artistic ability he offered him a post as botanical artist at the Royal Botanic Gardens, Kew. Banks paid Bauer's salary initially and only in later years did Bauer become an employee of the gardens directly. He continued as artist for the gardens until his death in 1840. During his years at Kew, Bauer became an outstanding student of botany and captured much of what he learnt in many of his drawings. He is one of the most technically sophisticated of all botanical artists and created some wonderfully detailed studies of plant structure using a microscope.

ARCHIBALD THORBURN
Greater horseshoe bat,
Rhinolophus ferrumequinum
Watercolour, 1919
414 x 527 mm

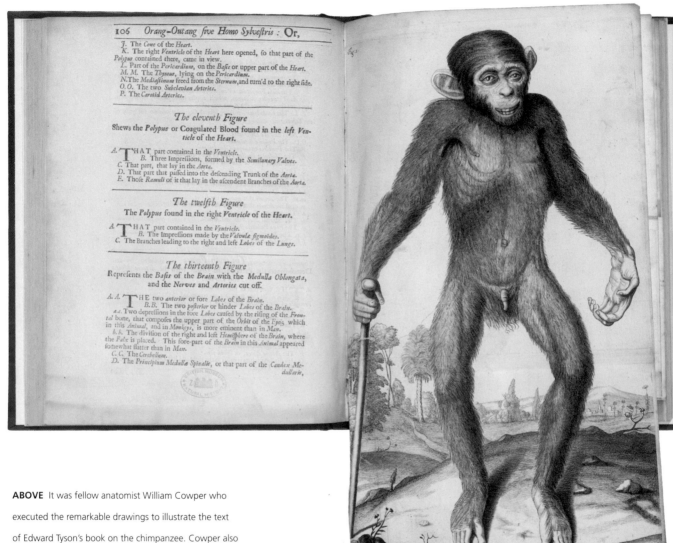

ABOVE It was fellow anatomist William Cowper who executed the remarkable drawings to illustrate the text of Edward Tyson's book on the chimpanzee. Cowper also contributed the chapter on the muscles.

WILLIAM COWPER
Chimpanzee, *Pan troglodytes*
Engraving, 1699
376 x 210 mm

France also had its fair share of celebrated flower painters and botanical illustrators. The Jardin du Roi was created in 1626 and remains the main botanical garden in Paris today, though its name changed to Jardin des Plantes after the French Revolution. Almost from its inception the garden employed artists. Claude Aubriet worked for many years at the garden and collaborated with the botanist Joseph Pitton de Tournefort on his *Elemens de Botanique* published in 1694. He also travelled with Tournefort for two years in 1700 in the Levant as his artist and continued to work in the garden on his return. In 1707 he became the Royal botanical painter. Others that followed Aubriet in this role included the Dutch-born artist Gerard van Spaendonck and his pupil the Belgian-born artist Pierre-Joseph Redouté.

The explosion in botanical art in the late eighteenth and early nineteenth centuries reflected Carl Linnaeus' direct impact on the discipline of botany. His taxonomic system based on the sexual characteristics of plants, first described in *Systema Naturae* in 1735, offered the artist a method of revealing the required facts about a species for classification purposes. The growth in botanical illustration had its counterpart in other areas of natural history. By the eighteenth century interest in the study of anatomy extended beyond the traditional groups of those studying medicine to those concerned with zoology. Already in the late seventeenth century French and English anatomists had begun directing their research to include comparative anatomy. These men saw all animal forms as being somewhat related and the purpose of studying their structure was to discover the hidden relations between animals. They also began to recognize that humans shared many anatomical traits with other animals. For much of the eighteenth century comparative anatomy was exclusively confined to studying anatomical structure and it was only with zoologists such as Georges Cuvier, Johannes Müller, Charles Bell and Richard Owen that the discipline was extended to include embryology, physiology and morphology.

The father of English comparative anatomy is Edward Tyson. His monograph *Orang-outang, sive Homo sylvestris: or, the Anatomy of a Pygmie compared with that of a Monkey, an Ape, and a Man*, published in 1699, remained a key work through to the nineteenth century. Tyson's book was a study of a chimpanzee, rather than the orang-utan of the title, that died soon after its arrival in London in 1697. Tyson managed to obtain the body to dissect and study it. The book is magnificently illustrated with eight engraved plates by fellow anatomist William Cowper and demonstrates for the first time how similar the structure of an ape is to a human. It was referred to by some of the leading naturalists of their day including Comte de Buffon and Georges Cuvier in France and Charles Darwin and Richard Owen in England. The chimpanzee dissected by Tyson was one of an increasing number of exotic animals being brought to Europe. As early as 1515 German painter Albrecht Dürer prepared

PINOKEPOC.

An Exact Figure of the
RHINOCEROS
That is now to be Seen in
LONDON.

Invented to Humffreyes COLE Esq.
Chief of The Hon.ble East India Com-
panys Factory at PATNA in the
Empire of The Great MOGUL for
the Favour he has done the Curious
in Sending it over to England.

Published October 10. 1739.

a wonderful woodcut of an Indian rhinoceros. Dürer was not fortunate enough to have seen the actual beast, alive or dead, and had to make his image from a brief sketch and a description. In 1739 the East India Company sent a rhinoceros to London where it was exhibited with tickets to view it costing two shillings and sixpence. The English artist Gerard van der Gucht made an engraving of it from a drawing by James Parsons who also produced an oil painting of the same animal.

The Enlightenment opened the way for enthusiastic naturalists and artists from all layers of society to pursue their interests. Amongst the more successful artists were a significant number of women. Sarah Stone worked as a natural history illustrator receiving commissions from Sir Ashton Lever, Sir Joseph Banks and other prominent collectors of natural history. She painted watercolours of many of the specimens brought back from expeditions from around the world, including those from Captain Cook's voyages. Another woman artist and excellent naturalist was Anna Children, known as Anna Atkins after her marriage. John Children, Anna's father, was a respected naturalist who provided an education for his daughter that included the broad spectrum of natural history and instilled in her an enquiring mind. Both father and daughter collaborated with the French naturalist Jean-Baptiste Lamarck for his *Genera of Shells*, the father translating the work and the daughter illustrating it. Anna developed an interest in photography and was instructed by the English astronomer Sir John Herschel in the cyanotype process of producing photograms. She was the first to publish a work that included cyanotype impressions of British algae and is today recognized as one of the pioneering natural history photographers.

By the second half of the eighteenth century the study of the history and composition of the Earth was taken up by ever increasing numbers of scientists. There was growing evidence that the age of the Earth was much greater than previously had been believed and new theories on the process of rock formation emerged. Two schools of thought developed: one that supported the biblical idea of a great flood and another that proposed volcanic activity as responsible for the layers of rock forming over long periods of time. Mapping the composition of the Earth and dating different strata by fossil evidence gained momentum through the early nineteenth century, and depicting the data in pictorial forms also made enormous advances. The English geologist William Smith was the first to produce a

Dictyota dichotoma
in the young state, &
in fruit.

LEFT Anna Atkins began publishing her book *British Algae: Cyanotype Impressions* in parts from 1843 and had completed it by 1853 with a total of 389 handmade photographic plates. Atkins' book was the first published work to use photography to replace the traditional method of illustration. She was also amongst the first botanists to study and publish on the subject of algae.

ANNA ATKINS
Dictyota dichotoma
or *Chondrus ciispus*
British Algae: Cyanotype Impressions, 1853
255 x 200 mm

geological map of Britain in 1815, which differs little from modern versions produced today. By the early nineteenth century emerging industrialists and empire builders regarded the natural sciences as something they could develop and exploit. The professional scientist was now slowly replacing the amateur who had been the dominant force in the eighteenth century. A noticeable shift also emerged amongst the artists. During the Enlightenment many skilled artists developed a great understanding of their subject and became excellent naturalists; by the mid-1800s there were scientists who were specialists within their own fields as well as being competent and sometimes exquisite artists. Three professionals that between them span the whole of the nineteenth century and represent this shift are William MacGillivray, Ernst Haeckel and Arthur Harry Church.

The Scottish-born naturalist William MacGillivray was an expert on birds and a gifted artist. Born in 1796 he was one of the first professional naturalists to pursue a career in the subject. He was assistant professor of natural history at Edinburgh University and later was appointed the curator of the museum of the Royal College of Surgeons in the same city. It was here that the young Charles Darwin, avoiding his medical lectures, would visit MacGillivray and his collections. In 1841 MacGillivray secured the position of professor of natural history at Marischal College, Aberdeen. Despite the professional aspect of his career he was very much a field naturalist, liking nothing better than to travel hundreds of miles on foot exploring and observing nature. Like Alexander Wilson before him, MacGillivray condemned the closet scientists who examined specimens without ever seeing the creature in its natural habitat. MacGillivray created striking portraits of birds and mammals, combining the natural beauty of the subject with fine accurate detail. He produced significant works of his own and contributed to others including the scientific text for Audubon's *Ornithological Biography*.

Ernst Haeckel was born in Potsdam, Prussia, in 1834. Influenced by physiologist Johannes Müller, his professor at Berlin University where he was studying medicine, Haeckel directed his later studies to zoology, specializing in marine life. He became professor of comparative anatomy at Jena University, a post he retained for 47 years. Haeckel worked in several areas of zoology and is best known for his work on radiolarians, which are single-celled protozoa found in plankton. He discovered many hundreds of new species and produced some stunning illustrations of marine creatures. Haeckel became the leading proponent of evolution in Germany, although he was more inclined towards French naturalist Jean-Baptiste Lamarck's idea of inherited acquired characteristics rather than Darwin's natural selection. He saw form as all-important and his illustrations reveal his understanding of nature as being governed by symmetry and organization.

Haeckel's artwork was something that was new to science and to the public at large. His illustrations sat very comfortably within the art and design movement of the late nineteenth and early

OPPOSITE This extraordinary compilation of various species of lizards features in Ernst Haeckel's work *Kunstformen der Natur* (Art Forms in Nature). The work is composed of 100 plates mainly of marine plants and animals. As a young man Haeckel considered a career as a painter, but he eventually chose to study science and thereby combined the two in his artwork.

ERNST HAECKEL
Various tropical lizards
Kunstformen der Natur,
1899–1904
Coloured lithograph
355 x 263 mm

OPPOSITE Hooker made sketches of the rhododendrons he discovered while travelling in the Himalayas and sent them to Walter Hood Fitch in London, who lithographed them for *The Rhododendrons of Sikkim-Himalaya 1849–1851*. Fitch did not see living examples of the rhododendrons but worked solely from the sketch, and sometimes the additional help of a dried specimen.

WALTER HOOD FITCH
Rhododendron fulgens
The Rhododendrons
of Sikkim-Himalaya,
1849–1851
Hand-coloured lithograph
495 x 350 mm

twentieth centuries. In 1899 Haeckel published the first in a series of prints called *Kunstformen der Natur* (Art Forms from Nature). It was these illustrations in particular that influenced so many artists, designers and architects in Europe.

Born in 1865, Arthur Harry Church is a fine example of an early twentieth-century scientist artist. After grammar school Church attended the University College of Wales, Aberystwyth. He then went to study at Queen's College and Jesus College, Oxford, after winning two scholarships offered to mature students. Church remained in Oxford for the rest of his life, becoming 'one of the least travelled botanists in Britain'.[1] Immediately after graduating with first-class honours in botany he was appointed to the botany department as a demonstrator. Church developed a style of artistry to demonstrate the internal structure of plants in their different stages of development. His artwork, though quite different from Haeckel, is without doubt recognizably influenced by Art Nouveau, which was at its height of influence when Church was producing illustrations for his unfinished work *Types of Floral Mechanism*.

The importance of having a vehicle through which to publish one's work was paramount for most naturalists and artists of the eighteenth and nineteenth centuries. The progress made in printing techniques and the invention of lithography and photography encouraged the growth of publishing of scientific monographs, travel books and regular productions of journals. In the last quarter of the eighteenth century many artists found work producing colour plates for the various popular magazines and journals as well as for the learned sectors of society. The most successful of these include William Curtis's *Botanical Magazine* first published in 1787 and which has continued, almost without interruption, to the present day. Zoological equivalents to the *Botanical Magazine* appeared, such as George Shaw's *Naturalist's Miscellany,* published from 1789 to 1813, and William Jardine's *The Naturalist's Library,* published from 1833 to 1861, which employed a series of well-known artists including Edward Lear and Prideaux Selby. Elsewhere in Europe notable publications such as *Flora Danica* in Denmark and *Hortus Sempervirens* in Germany included the work of some of the finest natural history illustrators of their time. In France the magnificent volumes by Redouté, amongst them *Les Liliacées* and *Les Roses*, are illustrated publications that have retained an importance to this day.

Not all publications were successful and the most famous of failures is probably Robert Thornton's *The Temple of Flora* published in 1799–1807. The work included some 30 large colour plates of flowers, which for the first time were set in landscapes depicting the natural habitat of the plant. The cost of the project was extraordinarily high and the work did not sell. The Napoleonic wars, Thornton explained, were to blame, resulting in taxing the 'moderately rich … to pay armed men to diffuse rapine, fire and murder, over civilized Europe'.[2]

Naturalists who travelled and wished to publish their reports often appealed to learned societies or the government of the day for help in defraying the costs. Only a few naturalists were successful, whereas most ventures into publishing succeeded through the hard work of raising subscriptions or underwriting the project themselves. The costs involved in producing colour plates could be astronomical. There was the long procedure of engraving copper plates, which is an intaglio rather than a relief printing process, so that a different press was used for plates from that used for the text. Then the engravings needed to be hand coloured, usually by families of colourists. For those naturalists who were not artistically gifted, a further cost would be the employment of an artist to prepare the original drawings for the engraver.

To be employed as the artist for a travelling scientist, and yet never travelling oneself and seeing a plant or animal in its native habitat, could present problems. Drawing from a description was difficult. Having a living specimen was an improvement but not always possible. For some artists a dried specimen was all that they had to go by in order to create a vibrant and animated drawing. Walter Hood Fitch, who for 43 years was the sole artist for the *Botanical Magazine,* also produced botanical illustrations for other naturalists and publications. His work was enhanced by the fact that he also did his own lithography, a style of printing that he mastered during his lifetime. Fitch produced the colour plates for Joseph Hooker's *The Rhododendrons of Sikkim-Himalaya,* published in 1849 to 1851. For some of the plates Fitch never saw a living example of the plant. He relied totally on sketches and dried specimens from Hooker and his own knowledge of plants, often drawing a composite image rather than one individual plant.[3]

Whilst Fitch produced splendid drawings of plants from specimens, John Gould was doing exactly the same with birds. Gould had started his career as a gardener but his real interest lay in birds. As a young man he learnt the craft of taxidermy and became so proficient in it that he set up his own business in London at the age of 20. Gould was also a skilled artist and studied all aspects of birds, becoming an authoritative and highly respected ornithologist. During his lifetime Gould produced over 40 volumes of books containing 3,000 illustrations of birds and mammals from around the world. He would often make sketches of birds that were then worked up to full watercolour drawings by one or several of his well-orchestrated team of artists. This team included artists such as Edward Lear, William Hart and Joseph Wolf. From the watercolour, Gould's lithographer, who until her death at the age of 39 was his wife Elizabeth, would copy the drawing onto the stone and a series of prints was made from them. The prints would then be sent to the family of colourists Gould employed.

Gould usually made his sketches from a skin or a stuffed bird which his artists would also have access to. When he was working on his *Birds of Europe* Gould travelled to several European

OPPOSITE John Gould's publishing output was prodigious and he produced magnificent works on birds from around the world. His scientific contribution to ornithology is unsurpassed, and the artwork for his books came from some of the most talented artists of the nineteenth century. Taking centre stage amongst all these works are his volumes of hummingbirds that comprise 418 hand-coloured plates.

JOHN GOULD
Green-throated carib,
Eulampis holosericeus
Plant: *Mandevilla sp.*
A Monograph of the Trochilidae, 1861
Hand-coloured lithograph
546 x 375 mm

OPPOSITE The Russian
artist Olga Makrushenko
constructs her work by using
airbrush overlay techniques.
A complicated process
that requires patience,
an exceptional eye for
detail and an excellent
understanding of what she
intends as an end result.
The technique brings a
translucent softness to her
depictions of nature.

OLGA MAKRUSHENKO
Shell and crab
Mixed media, 2000
80 x 100 mm

countries and visited the birds in zoos or in private collections. He also spent two years in Australia, which provided him a wealth of material for his volumes of *Birds of Australia*. However, for the vast majority of the drawings, Gould and his artists never saw the living bird. Gould was at the forefront of developing new techniques and one of his finest experiments was with the colourists for his *Monograph of the Trochilidae or Family of Humming-Birds*. In order to capture the iridescence of the feathers Gould laid fine gold leaf to the page, which was then painted over with transparent oil and varnish colours. The result was magnificent and has never truly been matched by any artist since.

Gould and his group of bird artists were an inspiration to succeeding generations of European artists. Many of them ended up living in England, attracted by Gould's influence, by the importance of the Zoological Society and by the fact that London had become the centre for ornithological publications. Also present in England at the time was a small group of wealthy naturalists, recognized today as the last of the great patrons of natural history art. Included in this group were Arthur Hay, 9th Marquis of Tweedale and 2nd Baron, Lionel Walter Rothschild.

Rothschild's boyhood interest in natural history developed into a passion by the time he was a young man. For his 21st birthday he was presented with a small museum building on his family estate into which he installed his collections from around the world. He sponsored several collecting expeditions including ones to the Galapagos Island that he leased for a period of eight years from 1897. He also built a magnificent library and commissioned artists to prepare drawings for several publications including his own, *Novitates Zoologicae*. Amongst the artists who found patronage from Rothschild were the Dutch-born John Gerrard Keulemans and Joseph Smit, the Danish Henrik Gronvold and the Prussian Joseph Wolf who had worked with John Gould. This whole group of artists worked on various projects sponsored by Rothschild as well as collaborating with other artists such as the Scottish-born Archibald Thorburn, another bird artist influenced by John Gould. Some, such as Smit and Gronvold, also worked for years in an unofficial capacity at the British Museum and all are recognized as fine zoological illustrators. However, none were untouched by the hidden influences of their era and many of their artworks can be viewed as artistic portraits of animals rather than the strictly zoological drawings required for scientific purposes.

Present day scientists probably rely on natural history art much less than previous generations did. This is partly because of changes in the study of science. Technological developments and new methods of visually recording a species have also made an impact on how natural history art is produced or required today. Taxonomy is not as fashionable as it once was and certainly fewer scientists are entering the discipline. Much of the systematic work in this field is carried out at a molecular level and emphasis is on the study of biodiversity and the processes that have shaped the world around us, together with the relationships between organisms and minerals. Photography now has an important role in the study of natural history and is often a favoured medium for field guides for help in identification; high-quality film and television series seem to have replaced journals and magazines for stimulating popular interest in natural history. Nevertheless, the audience for appreciating natural history art is greater than ever and there remain many artists who have opted to specialize in the subject. There are still artists who painstakingly study birds, animals and plants and produce wonderfully detailed portraits of what they observe. Elizabeth Butterworth and Olga Makrushenko are two such artists. And there are those who are still prepared to venture across the planet to pursue the elusive insect or bird, or to follow up a new discovery. One such contemporary example is Bryan Poole, who recently travelled to the Caribbean to seek out the purple-throated hummingbird and the heliconias the bird feeds upon. Poole is the latest in a long line of natural history artists who have travelled to the other side of the world to capture rare and interesting species on paper, a trend that started in earnest in the late 17th century and has continued to this day.

OPPOSITE Irises are some of the oldest of flowers to be represented in art. The bearded iris is a typical example of the many species and cultivars developed over the centuries and often depicted in Dutch and Flemish flower paintings. These ones by Maria Merian were produced on velum.

ABOVE This beautiful watercolour of fruit by Maria van Huysum could well be considered as a still-life painting rather than a natural history illustration. The van Huysum family included a great number of known artists many of whom were flower painters in the great Dutch tradition but others, such as Jacobus van Huysum, were botanical artists.

MARIA SIBYLLA MERIAN
Irises, *Iris* sp.
Watercolour and bodycolour
on vellum, c.1690s
336 x 268 mm

MARIA VAN HUYSUM
Plums, *Prunus* sp.
Watercolour, *c.* early 1700s
206 x 327 mm

LEFT Johann Hoch was primarily a portrait and landscape artist. By the mid 1700s he recognized a growing interest in natural history art as different organisms began to be studied systematically. Hoch produced hundreds of watercolour drawings of molluscs and crustacea and strove to capture the delicate varieties of colour in his subjects.

OPPOSITE Johann Christoph Dietzch was a landscape artist who also produced many flower paintings. Like other members of his artistic family he prepared his paintings on a dark-brown or black background, which resulted in a wonderful contrast between the ground and the bright colours used for the subject.

JOHANN GUSTAV HOCH
Collection of shells, clockwise from top left
Admiral cone,
Conus ammiralis
Episcopal or bishop cone,
Conus episcopus,
Imperial cone,
Conus imperialis,
Virgin cone, *Conus virgo*
Precious wentletrap,
Epitonium pretiosum
Watercolour, c.1771
230 x 364 mm

JOHANN CHRISTOPH DIETZCH
Cotton rose,
Hibiscus mutabilis
Bodycolour, c.1750
277 x 199 mm

OPPOSITE Velum, rather than paper, was a preferred medium for George Ehret. When executed by a skilled artist the effect of watercolours and bodycolour on vellum is stunning, as with this drawing of a magnolia. Ehret succeeds magnificently in bringing out the waxy texture of the petals of this flower.

GEORG EHRET
Magnolia,
Magnolia grandiflora
Watercolour on vellum,
1744
469 x 354 mm

RIGHT Ehret was the most well-known botanical artist during his lifetime. After he settled in London he was sought by many who owned large gardens and was invited to draw their favourite plants, one of which was probably this taro, which is native to India and Southeast Asia.

GEORG EHRET
Taro, *Colocasia esculenta*
Watercolour and bodycolour,
c.1740s
519 x 360 mm

RIGHT Georg Ehret's sketches are wonderful examples of his method of working and demonstrate his excellent botanical knowledge. Ehret drew many of the aloes growing in Chelsea Physic Garden, some of which were published in 1737. This one is native to the Cape area of South Africa.

OPPOSITE In the legend for this drawing Ehret explains that the plant, grown in Chelsea, flowered in 1738 and again in 1745.

GEORG EHRET
Aloe, *Aloe succotrina*
Watercolour and ink, c.1736
565 x 416 mm

GEORG EHRET
Sandbox tree, *Hura crepitans*
Watercolour and ink, c.1749
555 x 432 mm

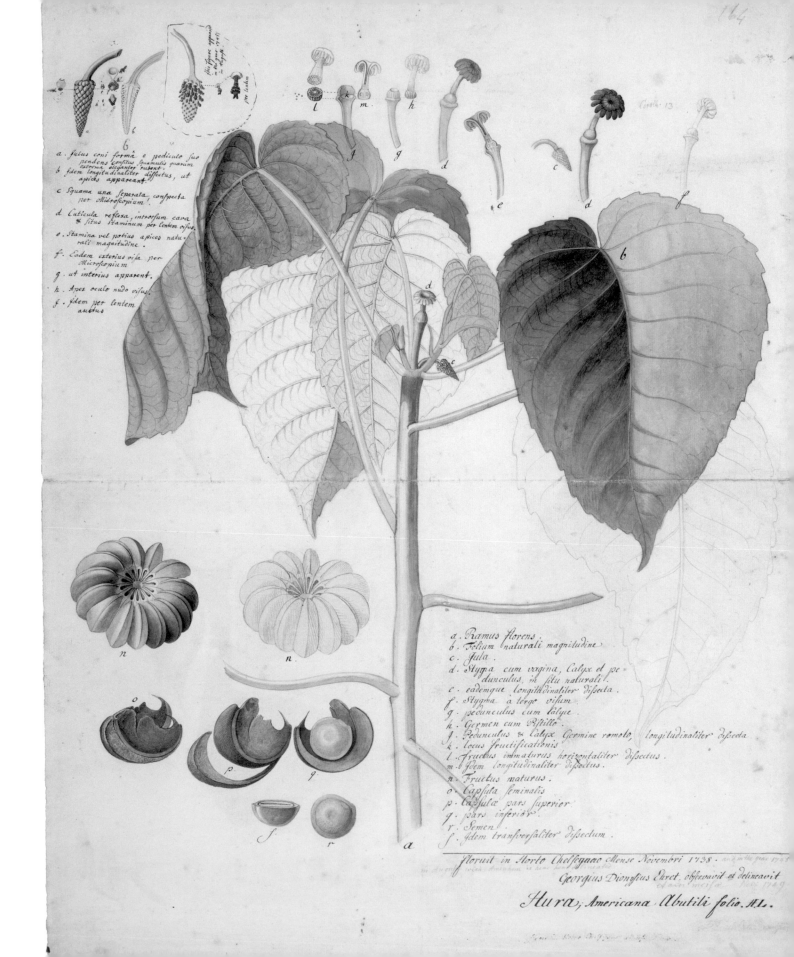

OPPOSITE The king protea is widely distributed in South Africa and is the national flower of the country. Its artichoke-like flower head is the largest of all proteaceae. This drawing by Franz Bauer was produced at the Royal Botanic Gardens, Kew. The flower would have been introduced into the garden by one of its collectors such as Francis Masson.

RIGHT Whilst Franz Bauer was a master at producing scientifically accurate drawings of plant parts viewed through a microscope, he was also able to create striking displays of single flowers that were seen as splendid works of art.

FRANZ BAUER
King protea,
Protea cynaroides
Watercolour, c.1800
523 x 370 mm

FRANZ BAUER
Hippeastrum sp.
Watercolour, c.1804
520 x 356 mm

RIGHT The bird of paradise
originates from South Africa
and was first grown in the
Royal Botanic Gardens, Kew
in 1773. Sir Joseph Banks
named the plant in honour
of Queen Charlotte, princess
of Mecklenburg-Strelitz.

FRANZ BAUER
Bird of paradise,
Strelitzia reginae
Watercolour, 1818
527 x 395 mm

Manihot Theveti,
Juca & Cassavi. I.B. 2. 794.

OPPOSITE Claude Aubriet was one of the earliest botanical artists to be employed at the Jardin du Roi in Paris. Like those who followed in his footsteps, Aubriet loved to produce his drawings on vellum, creating the wonderful luminosity that results from using the medium.

CLAUDE AUBRIET
Cassava, *Manihot esculenta*
Watercolour and bodycolour on vellum, early 1700s
423 x 303 mm

ABOVE LEFT AND RIGHT As professor of flower painting at the Jardin du Roi in Paris, Gerard van Spaendonck taught Pierre-Joseph Redouté, known as the 'Raphael of Flowers'. Spaendonck was a master at drawing on vellum and passed his expertise to his pupil.

GERARD VAN SPAENDONCK
Canary creeper, *Tropaeolum peregrinum*
Pithecellobium circinale
Both watercolour
Both 455 x 285 mm

Peacock Pheasant

OPPOSITE AND LEFT

Sarah Stone's watercolours of birds from around the world formed part of the collection of Sir Ashton Lever. The drawings were made from the 1780s and were important scientific records of then often unknown birds, in addition to being exquisite works of art. Stone painted many exotic birds that were brought back to England by travellers, collectors and from expeditions such as James Cook's *Endeavour* voyage. The golden pheasant is native to western China.

SARAH STONE
Grey peacock-pheasant,
Polyplectron bicalcaratum
Watercolour, c.1785
562 x 450 mm

SARAH STONE
Golden pheasant,
Chrysolophus pictus
Watercolour, 1788
531 x 436 mm

LEFT William Hamilton spent many years in Naples, Italy monitoring the activity of Mount Vesuvius. He communicated his observations to the Royal Society and on his return to England published a work on the subject that included a large collection of watercolour drawings. Hamilton employed Peter Fabris as the artist charged with translating his written descriptions into a visual media.

OPPOSITE William Smith produced amazing, ground-breaking geological maps in which each geological type is indicated by a different colour. A total of 20 different tints were used in the construction of the map.

PETER FABRIS
Plans of the top of Mount Vesuvius
Watercolour and bodycolour, 1776
450 x 320 mm

WILLIAM SMITH
Geological map of England, Wales and
part of Scotland
Hand-coloured engraving, 1815

LEFT The Cape gannet is native to the North Atlantic. The largest colonies breed around the coast of Britain, particularly in Scotland, and so William MacGillivray would have been familiar with this bird from an early age. This gannet, like all his bird illustrations, is drawn life size.

WILLIAM MACGILLIVRAY
Cape gannet, *Sula capensis*
Watercolour, c.1835
540 x 754 mm

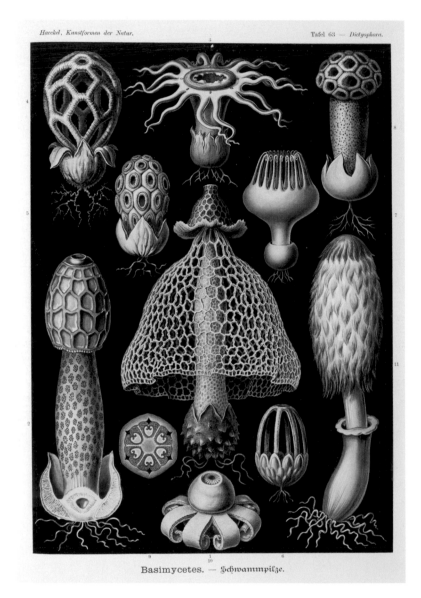

Haeckel, Kunstformen der Natur.

Tafel 63 — Dictyophora.

Basimycetes. — Schwammpilze.

LEFT AND OPPOSITE

Basidiomycota (left) is a
large phyla within the
sub-kingdom of fungi
and is often described
as filamentous fungi.
Blastoidea (opposite) are
fossils of a type of stemmed
echinoderm, an extinct
form of starfish. Haeckel
was obsessed with form
in nature and arranged
his subject on a page to
demonstrate the symmetry
and geometry of each
organism.

ERNST HAECKEL
Marine protozoa,
Acanthophracta radiolaria
Basidiomycota
Kunstformen der Natur,
1899–1904
Coloured lithograph
355 x 263 mm

ERNST HAECKEL
Echinoderm, *Cystoidea* sp.
Kunstformen der Natur,
1899–1904
Lithograph
355 x 263 mm

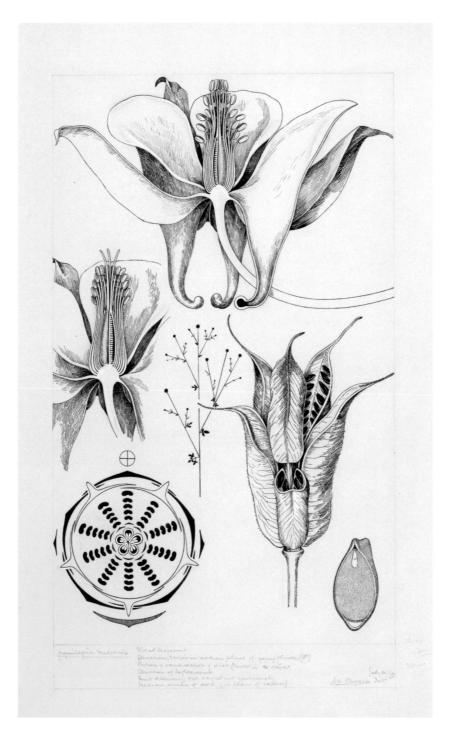

OPPOSITE AND LEFT

Arthur Harry Church's
brilliant watercolour
drawings of plants with
accompanying black and
white detailed diagrams are
considered revolutionary
in their approach to the
study of flowers. Church's
drawings were to illustrate
his botanical work *Types
of Floral Mechanism* of
which only the first part was
published, in 1908.

ARTHUR HARRY CHURCH
Columbine,
Aquilegia vulgaris
Watercolour and bodycolour,
1903
316 x 192 mm

ARTHUR HARRY CHURCH
Columbine,
Aquilegia vulgaris
Ink, 1903
316 x 192 mm

OPPOSITE *Temple of Flora* was intended as a tribute to the Swedish botanist Carl Linnaeus. Robert Thornton claimed that the 'most eminent British artists' were engaged in creating the plates. The true artists, however, were the dozen or more aquatint and mezzotint engravers he employed. These craftsmen combined their technique with stipple engraving, a method that made possible colour printing. The plates were then finished by hand.

RIGHT Redouté is the most famous flower painter to emerge from Le Jardin des Plantes in Paris. He produced exquisite plates for a whole range of botanical works but his best known is probably *Les Roses*, three volumes published in 1817–1824. Redouté was also responsible for introducing to France the technique of stipple engraving, creating tone by a mass of tiny dots, which he learnt from Francesco Bartolozzi when he visited England.

ROBERT THORNTON
Carnations, *Dianthus* sp.
Temple of Flora, 1799–1807
Hand-coloured engraving
570 x 450 mm

PIERRE JOSEPH REDOUTÉ
Rose, *Rosa* sp.
Les Roses, 1817–1824
Coloured engraving
535 x 340 mm

Rosa centifolia foliacea.   *Rosier à cent feuilles, foliacé.*

P.J. Redouté pinx.   *Imprimerie de Remond*   *Langlois sculp.*

RIGHT AND OPPOSITE As
a brilliant bird artist of the
first half of the nineteenth
century, Edward Lear was
sought by many to produce
paintings for various
published works. In 1832 he
produced his own volume
of parrots, *Ilustrations of the
Family of the Psittacidae*,
for which he not only did
the original watercolours
but also the lithographs for
the finished work. Lear also
contributed to Sir William
Jardine's Naturalist's Library,
of which the crowned
pigeon displayed opposite is
an example.

EDWARD LEAR
Alexandrine parakeet,
Psittacula eupatria
*Illustrations of the family of
Psittacidae*, 1832
Hand-coloured lithograph
555 x 365 mm

EDWARD LEAR
Western crowned pigeon,
Goura cristata
Watercolour, 1834
162 x 117 mm

PALÆORNIS CUCULLATUS.

Hooded Parrakeet.

205   30

Lophorus Coronatus.

RIGHT John Keulemans painted almost exclusively birds. He provided illustrations for several journals and magazines such as the *Ibis* and *The Proceedings of the Zoological Society*. He contributed to numerous books published at the end of the nineteenth and early twentieth century, including Walter Rothschild's *Extinct Birds* in 1907. This Bourbon crested starling is an example of one of the extinct birds for Rothschild's work.

JOHN KEULEMANS
Bourbon crested starling,
Fregilupus varius
Watercolour and bodycolour,
c.1900
380 x 274 mm

LEFT This colourful mandrill was painted by Keulemans during several visits to the London Zoological Garden, where he also painted other Apes and large monkeys.

JOHN KEULEMANS
Mandrill, *Mandrillus sphinx*
Watercolour and bodycolour, 1907
516 x 410 mm

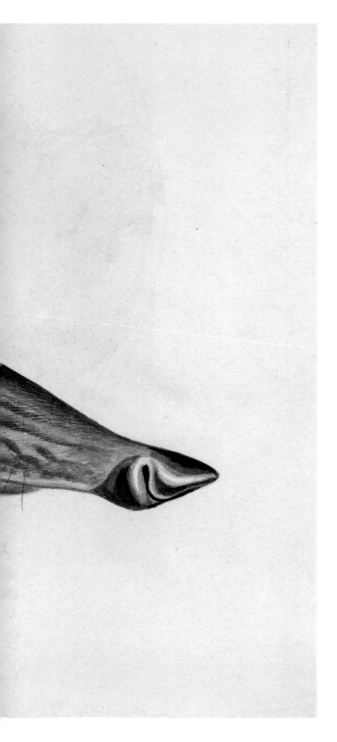

LEFT Like his fellow artist John Keulemans, Frederick Frohawk spent time at London Zoological Garden drawing the animals and birds resident there. This anteater was painted in 1902 and later published in Rothschild's *Novitates Zoologicae* in 1909.

ABOVE Henrik Gronveld was another European artist of the later nineteenth century who moved to England and painted for Lord Lionel Rothschild. He also provided illustrations for many well-known bird authors and their publications.

FREDERICK FROHAWK
South American coati,
Nasua nasua vittata
Watercolour, 1902
205 x 303 mm

HENRIK GRONVOLD
Olive ibis,
Bostrychia olivacea
Watercolour, c.1910
337 x 245 mm

RIGHT Archibald Thorburn prepared several watercolour drawings of whales for his work on British mammals including this one of a fin whale and a blue whale.

ARCHIBALD THORBURN
Fin and blue whales,
Balaenoptera physalus and
Balaenoptera musculus
Watercolour, 1920
409 x 561 mm

Pl. 43.

A. Thorburn
1920

Heliconia caribaea. ♂ Eulampis jugularis

4/100   Bryan Poole

OPPOSITE AND LEFT

These two engravings are stunning examples of plant animal relationships found in nature. The purple-throated hummingbird is sexually dimorphic. The male is larger with a short, straight bill; the female has a smaller body with a long, curved bill. This results in the one species of bird pollinating two distinct species of Heliconia with different shaped flowers.

BRYAN POOLE
Purple-throated humming bird, *Eulampis jugularis*
Heliconia, *Heliconia caribaea*
Aquatint etching, 2008
555 x 420 mm

BRYAN POOLE
Purple-throated humming bird, *Eulampis jugularis*
Heliconia, *Heliconia bihai*
Aquatint etching, 2008
555 x 420 mm

FOOTNOTES

Introduction
1. George Edwards, *Gleanings of Natural History,* Vol.1, 1758, x
2. Alexander Wilson, *American Ornithology*, Vol. 5, 1812, vi
3. William Bartram, *Travels*, 427
4. Alexander Humboldt, *Personal Narrative*, xxxv
5. Joseph Dalton Hooker, *Himalayan Journals*, 1854, vii

The Americas
1. Thomas Jefferson, *Notes on the State of Virginia*, 1785
2. William Baldwin to William Darlington, 20/8/1817, in Darlington, *Reliquiae Baldwinianae*
3. Alexander Wilson, *To the lovers of Natural history*, 6/4/1807, Proposal for publishing by subscription…*American Ornithology*
4. Alexander Wilson to Alexander Lawson, 4/4/1810, in Ord, 'Life of Wilson', lxxx

Australasia
1. *The Journals of Captain James Cook* (ed. Beaglehole), 1955, 1, cclxxxi
2. *The Journals of Captain James Cook* (ed. Beaglehole), 1955, 1. cclxxxii – cclxxxiii
3. John Ellis to Linnaeus in *Correspondence of Linnaeus*, ed. J.E.Smith, 1821, 1, 230
4. George Mackaness, *Letters from an Exile at Botany Bay, to his Aunt in Dumfries*, 1945, 11
5. Johann Goethe, 1817, in Mabberley, *Fedinand Bauer: the Nature of Discovery*, 1999, 123
6. David Mabberley, *Ferdinand Bauer: the Nature of Discovery*, 1999, 72

Asia
1. Ray Desmond, *The European Discovery of the Indian Flora*, 1992, 151
2. Ann Datta & Carol Inskipp, Zoology Amuses Me Much in, *The origins of Himalayan Studies*, 2004, 137

Africa
1. Homer Rutherford, *Sir Joseph Banks and the Exploration of Africa, 1788 to 1820*, 1952, 19
2. Georg Forster, *A Voyage round the World*, 1777, 1–2
3. William Harris, *Wild Sports of Southern Africa*, 1839, xviii
4. William Harris, *Wild Sports of Southern Africa,* 1839, xix

Europe
1. David Mabberley, *Arthur Harry Church: the Anatomy of Flowers*, 2000, 7
2. Robert Thornton, *The Temple of Flora*, Apology to Subscribers, 1807
3. Jim Endersby, *Imperial Nature: Joseph Hooker and the Practices of Victorian Science*, 2008, 125

FURTHER READING

Bowen, H V, Lincoln, M and Rigby, N (Editors), *The Worlds of the East India Company*. Boydell Press, Woodbridge, Suffolk, 2002.

Desmond, R, *The European Discovery of the Indian Flora*. Oxford University Press, Oxford, 1992.

De Vries-Evans, S, *Conrad Martens: On the Beagle and in Australia*. Pandanus Press, Brisbane, 1993.

Fan, Fa-ti, *British Naturalists in Qing China: Science, Empire and Cultural Encounter*. Harvard University Press, Cambridge, Massachusetts, 2004.

Gilbert, P, *John Abbot: Birds, Butterflies and Other Wonders*. Merrell Holberton, London, 1998.

Harris, W Cornwallis, *The Wild Sports of Southern Africa*. John Murray, London, 1839.

Humboldt, A, *Personal Narrative of Travels to the Equinoctial Regions of the New Continent* (translated by Helen Williams).
    Longman, London, 1818–1821.

Keynes, S, (Editor), *Ethiopian Encounters : Sir William Cornwallis Harris and the British Mission to the Kingdom of Shewa (1841–43),*
    Catalogue of Exhibition at The Fitzwilliam Museum. The Fitzwilliam Museum, Cambridge, 2007.

Kemp, A C, *Claude Gibney Finch-Davies 1875–1920 Observer, Student and highly skilled illustrator of Southern African birds*. Pretoria, 1976.

Lambourne, M, *John Gould – Bird Man*. Osberton Productions Ltd., Milton Keynes, 1987.

Mabberley, D, *Arthur Harry Church: the anatomy of flowers*. Merrell Holberton, London, 2000.

Mabberley, D, *Bauer: the nature of discovery*. Merrell Holberton, London, 1999.

Magee, J, *The Art & Science of William Bartram*. Pennsylvania State University Press, University Park, PA, 2007.

Stevenson, M (Editor), *Thomas Baines: An Artist in the Service of Science in South Africa, Accompanying the exhibition held at*
    Christie's, King Street, London 1–17 Sept 1999. Christie's International, Media Division, London, 1999.

Waterhouse, D M (Editor), *The Origins of Himalayan Studies: Brian Houghton Hodgson in Nepal and Darjeeling 1820–1858*. RoutledgeCurzon,
London, 2004.

BIOGRAPHICAL NOTES

Geographical location refers to place of birth.

Abbot, John 1751–1840
London, England
Collector and artist settled in Georgia.

Aldrovandi, Ulisse 1522–1605
Bologna, Italy
Collector and naturalist, established the
Botanical Gardens of the University of
Bologna.

Atkins, Anna 1799–1871
Tonbridge, Kent, England
Botanist and early photographer.

Aubriet, Claude 1665–1742
Chalon-sur-Marne, France
Artist and botanist.

Audubon, John James 1785–1851
Santo Domingo (now Haiti)
Artist and ornithologist who settled in USA.

Baines, Thomas 1820–1875
King's Lynn, Norfolk, England
Artist and explorer who settled in South
Africa.

Banks, Joseph FRS 1743–1820
London, England
Naturalist and president of the Royal Society
of London for 41 years, accompanied
James Cook on the HMS *Endeavour* voyage
1768–1771.

Bartram, William 1739–1823
Kingsessing, Philadelphia, USA
Naturalist and artist who travelled in
southeastern region of North America,
1773–1777.

Baudin, Nicolas 1754–1803
Ile de Ré, France
Naval officer and explorer who led the French
expedition to Australia, 1800–1803.

Bauer, Ferdinand 1760–1826
Feldsberg, Austria
Artist on several expeditions including
Australia, 1801–1803.

Bauer, Franz 1758–1840
Feldsberg, Austria.
Botanical artist at the Royal Botanic Gardens,
Kew, where he remained for 50 years.

Bernatz, Johann Martin 1802–1878
Speyer, Germany
Official artist on the expedition to Shewa,
Ethiopia, 1841–1843.

Bonpland, Aimé 1773–1858
La Rochelle, France
Botanist and explorer with Alexander von
Humboldt to South America.

Brunfels, Otto 1488–1534
Mainz, Germany
Botanist, considered the father of German
botany.

Butterworth, Elizabeth 1949–
Rochdale, England
Bird artist.

Catesby, Mark FRS 1683–1749,
Essex, England
Artist and natural history explorer and
collector in the American colonies.

Church, Arthur Harry FRS 1865–1937
Plymouth, England
Scientist and botanical artist.

Cook, James FRS RN 1728–1779
Marton, Yorkshire, England
Naval officer who circumnavigated the world
on three voyages.

Cowper, William FRS 1666–1709
Petersfield, Hampshire, England
Surgeon and human anatomist.

Darwin, Charles FRS 1809–1882
Shrewsbury, England
Scientist, sailed on the HMS *Beagle* 1831–
1836.

Dietzsch, Johann Christoph 1710–1769
Nuremberg, Germany.
Flower and landscape artist.

Ehret, Georg Dionysius FRS 1708–1770
Heidelberg, Germany
Botanical artist who settled in London,
England.

Finch-Davies, Claude Gibney 1875–1920
Delhi, India
Ornithologist and artist, served in the British
Army in South Africa.

Fitch, Walter Hood 1817–1892
Glasgow, Scotland
Botanical artist and lithographer, employed by
the Royal Botanic Gardens, Kew.

Fleming, John FRS 1747–1829
Scotland
Physician in the East India Company in
India late eighteenth and early nineteenth
centuries.

Flinders, Matthew 1774–1814
Donnington, Boston, Lincolnshire
Captain of the HMS *Investigator* on the British
expedition to Australia 1801–1803.

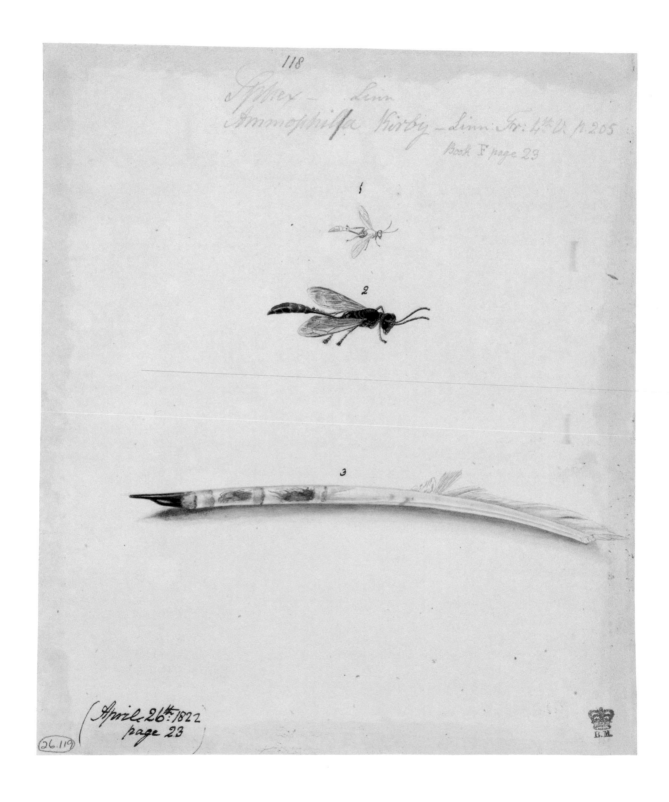

Forster, Georg 1754–1794
Nassenhuben, Prussia
Artist and assistant naturalist on the HMS *Resolution*, James Cook's second voyage.

Forster Johann 1729–1798
Dirschau, Prussia
Naturalist on James Cook's second voyage on HMS *Resolution*; father of Georg Forster.

Fountaine, Margaret Elizabeth 1862–1940
Norfolk, England
Entomologist and artist who travelled the world collecting butterflies.

Fuchs, Leonhard 1501–1566
Wemding, Germany
Physician and botanist.

Gesner, Konrad 1516–1565
Zurich, Switzerland
Naturalist.

Gould, John FRS 1804–1881
Lyme Regis, England
Ornithologist and artist.

Gronvold, Henrik 1858–1940
Praestö, Denmark
Natural history and bird artist.

Haeckel, Ernst 1834–1919
Potsdam, Prussia
Scientist and artist who specialized in marine organisms.

Hardwicke, Thomas FRS 1756–1835
Probably Cambridgeshire, England
Collector of natural history specimens and artwork from Asia.

Harris, William Cornwallis 1807–1848
Baptised Kent, England
Army officer in the East India Company, travelled in South Africa and led expedition to Shewa, Ethiopia 1841–1843.

Hamilton, William 1730–1803
London, England
Art collector and diplomat, studied vulcanology whilst in Naples.

Havell, Robert 1793–1878
Reading, England
Artist and printer who with his father produced Audubon's Birds of America.

Hernandez, Francisco 1517–1587
Toledo, Spain
Physician and naturalist who led the first scientific exploration to the New World.

Hoch, Johann Gustav 1716–1779
Reutlingen, Germany
Portrait, landscape and natural history artist.

Hodgson, Brian Houghton FRS 1801–1894
Cheshire, England
Naturalist, collector and ethnographer, civil servant in the East India Company in north India and Nepal.

Hooke, Robert FRS 1635–1703
Isle of Wight, England
Scientist, pioneer in the study of microscopy.

Hooker, Joseph Dalton FRS 1817–1911
Suffolk, England
Botanist and Director of the Royal Botanic Gardens, Kew, travelled in North India 1847–1849.

Humboldt, Alexander von 1769–1859
Potsdam, Prussia
Scientist and naturalist who travelled through South America from1799–1804.

Huysum, Maria van *fl.* 1750s
Amsterdam, Holland
Artist.

Keulemans, John Gerrard 1842–1912
Rotterdam, Holland
Bird painter who settled in London.

Lear, Edward 1812–1888
London, England
Artist, naturalist and writer.

Lesueur, Charles Alexander 1778–1846
Le Havre, France
Naturalist and artist who sailed on Baudin's expedition to Australia 1800–1803.

MacGillivray, William 1796–1852
Old Aberdeen, Scotland
Ornithologist, naturalist and artist.

Makrushenko, Olga
Moscow, USSR
Natural history artist.

Martens, Conrad 1801–1878
London, England
Artist who sailed on the HMS *Beagle* voyage, settled in Australia.

Masson, Francis 1741–1805
Aberdeen, Scotland
Plant collector and artist.

Mee, Margaret 1909–1988
Chesham, England
Botanical artist of the Amazon and Brazilian rainforest.

Merian, Maria Sibylla 1647–1717
Frankfurt, Germany
Artist and entomologist who travelled to Surinam.

Mutis, Jose 1732–1808
Cadiz, Spain
Led the botanical expedition in South America that lasted 25 years.

Nodder, Frederick Polydore *fl.* 1767–1800
Possibly Germany
Natural history artist.

Orta, Garcia De 1501–1568
Castelo de Vide, Portugal
Physician and botanist who settled in Goa, India.

Parsons, James FRS 1705–1770
Barnstaple, England
Physician and artist.

Parkinson, Sydney 1745–1771
Edinburgh, Scotland
Natural history artist on the HMS *Endeavour* voyage.

Poole, Bryan
New Zealand
Botanical artist and print-maker, living in London.

Port Jackson Painter *fl.* 1790s
Artist or artists from the First Fleet.

Raper, George 1769–1797
London, England
Naval officer and artist who sailed with the First Fleet 1778–1792.

Redouté, Pierre Joseph 1759–1840
Saint- Hubert, Belgium
Botanical artist at the Jardin du Roi, Paris

Reeves, John FRS 1774–1856
Essex, England
Tea inspector for the East India Company in China where he collected natural history specimens and artwork.

Rothschild, Lionel Walter FRS 1868–1937
London, England
Zoologist and patron of collectors and artists.

Roxburgh, William 1751–1815
Ayrshire, Scotland
Superintendent of the Calcutta Botanic Garden, commissioned botanical artwork of Asian plants.

Royle, John Forbes FRS 1798–1858
Cawnpore, India
Surgeon and naturalist served in the East India Company at Saharunpore Garden

Russell, Patrick FRS 1727–1805
Edinburgh, Scotland
Physician and naturalist, served in the East India Company, India.

Schomburgk, Robert FRS 1804–1865
Freyburg, Prussian Saxony
Explorer and naturalist; travelled in British Guiana.

Smith, William 1769–1839
Oxfordshire, England
Geologist and geological cartographer.

Solander, Daniel FRS 1733–1782
Norrland, Sweden
Naturalist, a pupil of Linnaeus and assistant to Joseph Banks on the HMS *Endeavour* voyage.

Spaendonck, Gerard van 1746–1822
Tilburg, Holland
Botanical artist.

Stone, Sarah c.1760–1844
place of birth unknown, lived as an adult in London, England
Natural history artist.

Talbot, Dorothy 1871–1916
England
Artist and botanical collector who travelled in Nigeria.

Thorburn, Archibald 1860–1935
Edinburgh, Scotland
Natural history artist who specialized in birds.

Tonge, Olivia 1858–1949
Glamorgan, Wales
Artist who travelled in India.

Tyson, Edward 1650–1708
Somerset, England
Scientist who is known as the father of British comparative anatomy.

Wallace, Alfred Russel FRS 1823–1913
Usk, Monmouthshire, Wales
Naturalist and collector who travelled to South America and the Malay Archipelago.

Wallich, Nathaniel FRS 1786–1854
Copenhagen, Denmark
Physician and botanist in India.

Watling, Thomas 1762– unknown
Dumfries, Scotland
Artist, sent as a convict to the penal colony of Port Jackson, Australia in 1791.

Webber, John 1751–1793
London, England
Official artist on Captain Cook's third and final voyage, 1776–1780.

White, John c.1540–c.1593
England
Artist who travelled with Richard Grenville to Roanoke in 1585.

Wilson, Alexander 1766–1813
Paisley, Scotland
Ornithologist and bird artist who settled in USA.

Wolf, Joseph 1820–1899
Münstermaifeld, Germany
Wildlife illustrator and artist.

Young, William 1742–1785
Kassel, Germany
Plant collector in the American colonies, appointed Queen's Botanist in 1763.

INDEX

Page numbers in *italic* refer to artwork plate labels.

JOHN REEVES COLLECTION
Blue magpie,
Urocissa erythrorhyncha
Watercolour, *c.* 1820s
445 x 385 mm

ACKNOWLEDGEMENTS

A sincere thanks goes to the publishing team at the Natural History Museum who have been a delight to work with and who made the whole process of this production as smooth and painless as possible. A very special mention must be made of David Mackintosh, the designer, whose excellent work is displayed here for all to see, and with whom it has been a pleasure to work. I would also like to thank the staff of the Natural History Museum: in the Library, Lisa di Tommaso, Sam Gare, Natalie Pope, Armando Mendez and Andrea Hart for their hard work in locating artwork; in the photographic unit, Pat Hart, for producing the images for the book; and to the scientific staff in Botany and Zoology departments for help in identification of species. In addition to the above I would like to thank Mike Schlesinger, Chris Mills and Celia Coyne for correcting and making suggestions to the manuscript.